TIME WARRIOR

How to defeat procrastination, people-pleasing, self-doubt, over-commitment, broken promises and chaos

TIME WARRIOR

How to defeat procrastination,
people-pleasing, self-doubt, over-commitment,
broken promises and chaos

Steve Chandler

MAURICE BASSETT

books for athletes of the mind

Time Warrior: How to defeat procrastination, people-pleasing, self-doubt, over-commitment, broken promises and chaos.

Maurice Bassett
P.O. Box 839
Anna Maria, FL 34216-0839

MauriceBassett@gmail.com
www.MauriceBassett.com

Editing by Kathryn McCormick and Chris Nelson
Cover art by SeeSaw Designs

Steve Chandler's website:
www.SteveChandler.com

ISBN-10: 1-60025-037-8
ISBN-13: 978-1-60025-037-8

Library of Congress Control Number 2011903186

First Edition

To Kathy

Contents

Contents (continued)

Contents (continued)

Contents (continued)

Acknowledgments

Kathryn Anne Chandler for everything.
Steve Hardison for the ultimate in coaching.
Deuce Lutui for the internal commitment.
Barbie Gummin for the life coaching connection.
Maurice Bassett for the fearless club.
Michael Neill for the academy of super coaches.
Brandon Craig for sales mastery.
Rich Litvin for the confidence salon.
Todd Musselman for words and music.
Dusan Djukich for straight line leadership.
Fred Knipe for doctoring and cabaret performing.
Sam Beckford for being the small business millionaire.
Terry Hill for the two guys quartet.
Peter and Victoria Sykes for the music school.
Regena Thomashauer for the womanly arts school.
Stephen McGhee for modeling ascendance.
Rob Owen for results now.
Ken Webb for a holly jolly Christmas.
Colin Wilson for the books.
Byron Katie for the work.
George Will for the review.
Bruce Lee for the inspiration.

Publisher's Preface

Are you a "time tracker"? Most of us are—it's all too easy to have a sense of limitation with respect to time. We hastily divide the day into sixty-minute "slices" and then watch those slices slip away one by one. Then we wonder, "Where did the day go?"

Time Warrior gives us a revolutionary, non-linear approach for dealing with time, as bold as it is fresh and new. Forget whatever "guidebooks" you may have read on time management or personal productivity. *Time Warrior* is much more than tips and tricks. Steve Chandler has given us an invitation—as well as a challenge—to become something far greater than we are now. To become, in essence, a "style tracker" rather than a "time tracker." Tracking your cognitive *style* is what makes you a Time Warrior, for only your unique cognitive style can liberate you from the treadmill of linear, limited time.

This book takes you on a 101-chapter journey intended to transmute the base metals of ordinary linear time-consciousness into the gold of the Time Warrior's non-linear vision. You will learn to create for yourself a newfound and more powerful cognitive style that will make time tracking, multi-tasking and other clock-subservient behaviors an unsavory and distant memory.

Time Warriors arrange the "chaos" around them by slowing down—way, way down—and then letting go of people-pleasing, approval-seeking and every shade of mood-based and future-based thinking. Their battle is for style integrity, for the synchronization of cognitive style with personal purpose.

Technological and cultural contaminants must be struck down throughout the day if one is to create and shape her day the Time Warrior way. Then, when all is struck down, the Time Warrior is free to choose her own path, taking one step at a time, completing every project and finishing every task one at a time, putting her world under contribution instead of being "put upon" throughout the day.

Chandler himself is a Time Warrior. Having written more than thirty books, of which more than a million copies have been sold, we are inclined to watch closely as he shows how Time Warriors are not unhinged by irrelevancies throughout the day—or conditioned or discomfited by external circumstances—having found in their own cognitive style a fearless partner in joyful day-creation.

Time Warrior is a serious call to ownership, a serious call to own your own day.

Maurice Bassett

Introduction

What is non-linear time management?

Non-linear time management is a commitment to action in the present moment. It's looking at a task and choosing NOW or "not now." If it's not now, it's got to be NEVER, or placed in a time capsule that has a spot on the calendar and therefore out of the mind.

The mind must remain clear and empty of all future considerations.

In non-linear time management there is no line extending from my mind into the future. No tapeworm of unfinished business coming out of my body.

Non-linear time management is best expressed by Elvis Presley when he sings, "It's now or never, come hold me tight."

The old-fashioned time management programs had a huge, burdensome focus on the future. The line of tasks stretched out forever into the future. It was fear-based and it was overwhelming to have so much of a future to carry around with you.

It resulted in massive, pathological procrastination. Everything got put off in the name of perfectionism. Nothing was bold or reckless anymore. Therefore there wasn't much astonishing success happening for the world-weary practitioner.

But when I teach people to go non-linear, a strange thing happens. New life and energy come in. When they open their emails they don't get to save them for later. They have to deal with them if they open them. Like little attackers in a computer game, there is no longer anywhere to hide. Life becomes a great game and everything is handled right now on the spot.

All fear comes from picturing the future. Putting things off increases that fear. Soon we are nothing but heavy minds weighing down on weary brains. Too much future will do that.

Only a warrior's approach will solve this.

A warrior takes his sword to the future. A warrior also takes his sword to all circumstances that don't allow him to fully focus.

I am a coach by profession, and when I work with a client who is "overwhelmed" with too much to do and not enough time to do it I will often ask them to give me an example of one of the things they are burdened by every time they think about it. The client will give me an example and we will do that thing right now. The client is amazed. The only thing missing in this client's life was a bias for action.

Most people think too much. Then they compound that problem by studying the feelings that come up for them as a result of that thinking.

All this time that they spend thinking and feeling they could have been taking action. In a non-linear way.

Linear time starts with your birth and ends (at the end of the line) with your death. Along that long linear line it's just one damn thing after another. Then the lights go out. What was the point?

Non-linear time management stops all that weary nonsensical treading on the road to one's destiny.

Rather than inching along horizontally you must simply rise up. Your life can now become vertical. Now you don't postpone challenges, you rise to them. You become a warrior. And it works.

How, exactly, does it work? This book will show you exactly how it works.

Steve Chandler
Phoenix, Arizona
January 2011

The successful warrior
is the average person
with laser-like focus.

Bruce Lee

Chapter 1

Why not do something with your time?

Bruce Lee identified the warrior as an average person with laser-like focus.

But what if the average person *has* no focus, laser-like or otherwise?

We average people are usually too diffuse to connect with anything. We scatter our forces. We try to please. We unconsciously change ourselves every day while desperately trying not to. We try to cling to the foolish consistency known as a permanent personality, but it never holds. One foul mood sweeps in and no one recognizes us.

Or a buoyant mood overcomes us and we get our hopes up. Then the mood fades and we become someone else again.

Who are we? Buoyant or foul-tempered? We fight to regain control and come in somewhere in the middle. We don't want people to be afraid of us, but neither do we want them to expect too much. All our personalities, therefore, are crafted from the most hair-raising mediocrity. It's the middle way. Team Mediocre.

All the energy it takes to try to hold this mediocre personality—this one consistent person—together could have been used to create something.

But who knew? I mean really, when you were growing up, who told you that?

You had a hard enough time dealing with Santa not being real. How were you to handle *yourself* being a total fabrication?

Chapter 2

How to keep your soul alive

*To know what you prefer, instead of humbly saying
'Amen' to what the world tells you to prefer, is to have
kept your soul alive.*

Robert Louis Stevenson

When I accept the role of time warrior, I will seek first
to keep my soul alive. Instead of what most people do.
They try to keep their fake identity alive.

As warrior (not worrier) I will wake up and create my
day based on how I prefer to *serve* this world. And I can
do this in any format, including washing dishes at the
hotel, if I do it with enough love, energy and humor.

People who do "lowly" jobs with love and energy find
themselves being promoted and offered other "better"
jobs very quickly. Because they understand what Robert
Frost meant when he said, "The way out is *through*."

Other people "stuck" in "lowly jobs" where they
imagine they are being unjustly "nickeled-and-dimed"
are always looking for a way out. Never seeing that the
way out is through.

A warrior does not "get out."
A warrior goes through.

Chapter 3

No, you'll never find time

You will never 'find' time for anything,
if you want time you must make it.

Charles Buxton

And just how do you make time?

It's made in your mind. By slowing down. Paradoxically. By creating your day. By being ruthless. With great swings and swipes of your samurai sword. You develop a brutal grace. Cutting out the unnecessary.

Instead of letting your calendar abuse you, and letting people use you.

Why do you let all these other people clutter up your day? Because you want to please them? Because you believe their approval is everything?

I have never seen a greater time-waster than people-pleasing. The nervous habit of scurrying around trying to win the approval of others. Answering all their emails the minute they come in, taking their every call, fulfilling every request... interrupting myself and my own dream over and over.

There's no time left for achievement. For creation.

On this matter of people-pleasing, I learned more in Byron Katie's nine-day school than in any other nine-day period in my life by a factor of about a thousand. Katie says, "God spare me from the desire for love, approval and appreciation. This would be my one prayer because the answer to this prayer brings the end of time and space."

That's non-linear time management in a nutshell.

So Katie, what is there when there is no time and space? She says there is energy, love's pure energy. She says, "It's the energy of pure unlimited mind, set free in all its power and goodness."

A time warrior is a peaceful warrior but a warrior still. Peacefully taking a sword to all those negative, frightening, depressing thoughts that are automatically believed... so that a great, timeless, active day can be created. A day with no time in it unless you want to make some.

The basic difference between an ordinary man and a warrior is that a warrior takes everything as a challenge while an ordinary man takes everything either as a blessing or a curse.

Carlos Castaneda

Chapter 4

What do I do when I'm overwhelmed?

This is not a book about time management because a time warrior does not manage time. A time warrior goes to war with (challenges and cuts away) all the beliefs that create linear time.

What's left is timeless.

When we imagine (perceive) that we are overwhelmed by outside events (or options, or tough choices, or situations, or ways of making money, etc.) it is an illusion, because the brain doesn't even function that way.

Only a thought believed can produce a feeling of overwhelm.

In a simple life in which you only do what's in front of you, there can be no overwhelm, ever.

That life is yours to create. And it never just arrives, it must be created.

Chapter 5

"Violence" is sometimes quite good

The "violence" in the words "time warrior" was intended. For although the work you do can be slow and easy, you must pull out your sword ahead of time to carve out periods of space and silence.

Devoted time.

It's your war against interruption and distraction. Because if you can bring gentle, sustained focus to a task, you'll never regret the results.

As my friend and colleague Dusan Djukich says in his marvelous book, *Straight Line Leadership*, we stop. We start something and then we stop. When Dusan coaches his clients his recommendation is this: stop stopping.

The more space we open up for ourselves the more problems we solve. The faster we achieve our goals. The great philosopher Voltaire observed, "No problem can withstand the assault of sustained thinking."

The key word in Voltaire's observation is "sustained." We don't sustain. We don't take long, thoughtful, sustained walks. We don't sit quietly in space and solitude until a problem disappears (which it would) because we are too busy.

Or, we think we are. Same thing.

We think we're busy, especially today, with the way our "phones" hook us up to the whole nagging planet. We are so connected now! We never have to be alone again!

This is good?

In most ways, it is. It's fun and exciting when I sit in my Arizona office and get an urgent text from a client in Scotland. The phone beeps and I grab it and check it.

But what happens when I do that? I interrupt my meditative train of thought and it might have been a train that was taking me to a HUGE breakthrough solution to a major challenge. Beep, beep, beep! And I stop. I am *on to* something beautiful if only I would continue, but I stop.

Are you a good piano player? No? But you took lessons, once, didn't you? Yes? What happened?

"I stopped."

Have you ever looked back on your life and wondered what would have happened if you hadn't stopped? Piano, a foreign language, studying a certain subject, a distant love, *anything*.

Management and efficiency studies in the work place tell us that one hour of uninterrupted time is worth three hours of time that is constantly interrupted.

Or, as the old saying says, winners focus, losers spray.

So the warrior element in how you relate to time is how "violent" a swordsman you are going to be before your day begins. How much uninterrupted time will you carve out for yourself? Will you be a true time warrior? Because if you will, you'll love your timeless time.

You'll be amazed at what you can create when time is not an issue.

I travel differently now than I used to. When I go on a speaking trip I build extra time and space into my journey. In the past, it was different. I raced around like most everyone else, booking flights that left right after my speech was over. Running through airports, chattering on my phone in taxicabs, coaching people on the fly! It was a chaotic storm of a life. It was frantic and even unfulfilling, always unfinished and incomplete. I was *racing against time*, trying to get ahead of myself, trying to break the sound barrier so that I could get into my own future.

Do you know people who live that way? They try to live faster than the speed of sound. And then they wonder why they never hear anybody.

What couldn't they hear? They were going so fast they couldn't hear the universe whispering to them. What was the universe saying? The universe was saying "yes" to whatever they might ask for.

Joyce Carol Oates wrote a fascinating book on boxing that she was creative enough to call On Boxing. She is a prolific and accomplished novelist who has always had a fascination with the sweet science of boxing. In her book she studies the undefeated heavyweight champion of the world, Rocky Marciano. Marciano was a rather extreme example of what happens when you become enough of a time warrior to place sustained, relentless, uninterrupted focus on one single thing you are seeking to accomplish. Here's what Ms. Oates wrote:

"Marciano was willing to exclude himself from the world, including his wife and family, for as long as three months before a fight. Apart from the grueling physical ordeal of this period and the obsessive preoccupation with diet and weight and muscle tone, Marciano concentrated on one thing: The upcoming fight. Every minute of his life was defined in terms of the opening second of the fight. In his training camp the opponent's name was never mentioned in Marciano's hearing, nor was boxing as a subject discussed. In the final month Marciano would not write a letter since a letter related to the outside world. During the last ten days before a fight he would see no mail, take no telephone calls, meet no new acquaintances. During the week before the fight he would not shake hands. Or go for a ride in a car, however brief. No new foods! No dreaming of the morning after the fight! For all that was not *the fight* had to be excluded from consciousness. When Marciano worked out with a punching bag he saw his opponent before him, when he jogged he saw his opponent close beside him, no doubt when he slept he "saw" his opponent constantly—as the cloistered monk or nun chooses by an act of fanatical will to "see" only God."

Sportswriters studied Marciano's style in the ring for years, trying to analyze his amazing success. No one ever defeated him. But what they didn't study was what a warrior he was *in preparation*. To exclude everything that was not the fight from consciousness was where the real fight was won.

A warrior of time is like Rocky Marciano. He is also a spiritual seeker in that he is willing to begin his life over each morning. And that secret is to truly begin all of life all over again each day. Instead of thinking in long-term, linear patterns, the warrior tears the fabric of time wide open.

Yes this is spiritual.

St. Francis de Sales wrote: "I am glad you make a fresh beginning daily; there is no better means of attaining... than by continually beginning again."

Chapter 6

Situations don't cause feelings

Sometimes people think radical, innovative time management is something they are going to have to get into later. Right now, they are dealing with a difficult situation. And they are feeling overwhelmed.

They don't realize something important.

Situations—even "dramatic" situations like bankruptcy, divorce, death and economic recession—cannot directly cause a feeling of any kind until the brain interprets and creates a story about said situation.

Sadness, depression, frustration, upset, and anxiety can only be produced by seeing a situation and then producing an interpretation of it and then believing that interpretation. So, therefore, you and I can only be overwhelmed by our thoughts about something, never the thing itself.

I keep daydreaming a scene I'd like to put in a book or movie. A mad man (Me? Why not?) lives in a mental ward. (Me? It fits.) Each day they let this man into the recreation room. He's in his pajamas. He sits down at the circular table. The attendant gives him a big blank pad of paper and a box of crayons. He takes out the crayons and draws the head of a monster. He stares at the monster, screams, and runs out of the room.

The whole thing looks funny to the attendant. It looks, shall we say it... insane. The poor mad man is scaring himself to death!

And crazy as that looks, we ourselves do that each day. We use our crayons (our imagination) to scare ourselves instead of to create.

One person sees rain and gets sad because of their story about rain that they are believing. ("It's gloomy. It means I'll be cooped up.") Another person sees rain and gets happy because of their story about the rain. ("It's refreshing. It's romantic. It grows my garden.") It's the same rain in both cases. Rain has no meaning until we add it.

Each person believes the rain is causing the feeling, but in neither case is the rain causing the feeling. In both cases it is the thought believed that is causing the feeling. We add the meaning ourselves. Something happens, and we add the meaning of it. Circumstance carries no meaning by itself.

Rain has no meaning. That's the beauty of the rain.

Chapter 7

A pessimist is a human joke

*We possess such immense resources of power
that pessimism is a laughable absurdity.*

Colin Wilson
Poetry and Mysticism

But where are those immense resources today? They cannot be accessed because today I am nursing my resentments.

Did I put it on the top of my "to do" list to nurture my smallest resentments? Do I consider going out, purchasing gauze and dressings for my psychic wounds—wounded pride, wounded ego, and all of that? Can't I see that these are all the things that shut me down? All the things that hide who I really am?

When I'm shut down like that I am out of action and my life is getting worse. Because I am out of action. But now there's a crisis. And in a crisis? In a true emergency? I rise up and you see me at my best!

So the overriding question of life is: Who will produce the crisis? Fate or me? How will I now live?

Waiting for outside emergencies and challenges to wake me up?

Or living another way? The way of the warrior.

Chapter 8

Why am I not sticking with my goals?

There is a famous story circulating around the world right now about a professional football player named Deuce Lutui. I'll have a lot more to say about Deuce in a future book I'm writing about coaching. For now you can get his amazing story at www.tbolitnfl.com. Please go there and read.

You'll find that Deuce turned his whole professional life around in a single day. He was working with my own Jedi master coach Steve Hardison (www.theultimatecoach.net) and declared himself to be, from that moment, from that heartbeat forward, the best offensive lineman in the NFL. He sent a text to Hardison with the acronym at the bottom: TBOLITNFL.

From that moment forward Deuce began playing differently. Living differently. He had come into pre-season football camp that year out of shape and overweight and disgruntled about his contract. He even called himself, looking back, "the Lindsay Lohan of pro football."

But once he declared his commitment on the inside, everything changed on the outside. He began playing like a man possessed. Announcers and sportswriters noticed. Other NFL players noticed:

"Deuce, what's gotten into you?"

Notice how powerful that question is. What's gotten into you? Not "Where are you headed?" Because Deuce's commitment was internal, not external. It did not depend on any outside factor or circumstance for him to begin playing and living as the best offensive lineman in the NFL. The whole point of the "goal" (actually a transformation) is that it was internal. It was totally up to him, not others.

He even had a short version of it. He called it: "I am."

If I AM something, I don't have to worry about anything happening in my favor in the future. It's already in me. Like my heart.

Looking back on my own dysfunctional life, I remember I would always set goals and then worry about them.

Then I realized everything was distended, out into the future. No wonder it was hard for the mind to hold on to.

So I made my goals shorter. Short-term "process goals" that I always finished and felt good about. I no longer thought about long-term goals. Therefore I never had to worry about "sticking with" something.

I wrote on my wall: Be brief. Be swift. Be effective.

Process goals encouraged me to enjoy the present moment. They are brief and achievable. I set up process goals and fun tasks and projects so that I never had to worry about future "outcome" goals.

The best futures get created in the present moment.

The worst thing is to be so worried about your future that you miss *creating it* right now—right here in the present moment. The only place it can ever be created. (Worth repeating, obviously.)

Process goals should be very precise. Two miles. Twenty-one pushups. Thirty minutes writing the new book. Five sales calls. $23,000 in sales proposals this week.

But... isn't that reducing life to the mundane? "Mundane" is a story that we add to very interesting and exciting small challenges. Adding a negative word like "mundane" to a colorful task is like painting a wildflower with black paint.

Only you yourself can fire you up. Challenge yourself more. Get creative.

Create projects and small adventures that lead you to the grand vision you want. None of this has to be experienced as pressure. Ever. The great quarterback Fran Tarkenton used to say, "If it's not fun you're not doing it right."

So forget considerations of "happiness" and just get into action. Happiness is something you notice you are feeling later... *after* you've been in action for a while. It's not something to worry about ahead of time. And don't hold your happiness hostage to the achievement of a long term goal. If you do that, your happiness is always in the future. Always a hostage. And the future doesn't exist right now, does it? Notice that Deuce Lutui's commitment is to be the best offensive lineman in the NFL *right now*. (How else could he access that commitment? One cannot access the future until it is thoroughly internalized!)

Don't create your year, create your day. Figure out the perfect day and then live it. The year will take care of itself. So will your life.

Chapter 9

Get as small as you can, now smaller

A time warrior removes her sword and dismembers procrastination.

And this may be the most important thing she's ever learned about winning the war against procrastination: she can always start small. Start small, and the smaller the better.

The mind makes all future tasks big and scary. So we procrastinate.

Even little things, when we imagine doing them in the future, get distorted and take on frightening proportions.

Objects in the mirror of the future appear **larger** than they really are. Because the imagination, when it ventures into the future, always finds the worst case. No wonder we procrastinate! Thinking and imagining the worst case scares us into putting everything off.

Action is the answer.

But not always big action. Try three minutes. Give your task three minutes of your time. (You can address 40 neglected things in two hours this way.) Small actions. Any tiny action.

And make sure the action is effortless, too. As they say in Zen, *effortless effort*. Always the best. Three minutes then walk. Quit. Bail. Walk away. Barefoot.

(If you can, that is. But my experience is that nine times out of ten I get excited by how easy this thing really was all along. It was just masquerading as big and scary seen through the lens of my worst case future.)

Now knowing I only have a three-minute commitment I just *do the thing* I was procrastinating about! I just make that a policy!

Just do that one thing—you know what it is—it's the thing you're thinking about right now.

Don't think in terms of patterns. None of this: "I always" or "I never" because those globalizing thoughts will never serve you. They will scare you and make you a pessimist. Keep your life creative and simple: what needs to be done now in these three minutes? That's all you ever need to ask, and you'll never have anything like procrastination bother you again.

Chapter 10

Time to change the world

It's what you do with your time that frees up more time and draws life into your world.

Are you doing what you're doing right now better than you have ever done it? Be truthful. Or is it just "as good as" or "good enough?" The "good enough" stuff we do is **not good enough** for the time warrior.

My favorite American philosopher is Ralph Waldo Emerson who once observed, "If you write a better book, or preach a better sermon, or build a better mousetrap than your neighbor, the world will make a beaten path to your door."

Do you want to succeed at something? Good work *right now* will help you do that. Most people want to start by improving how they "market" their services. Maybe a new website, or a better network of affiliates. But most of the time that's not where the answer lies.

The answer is in the work itself.

Let's slow down. Let's write a better book, preach a better sermon or build a better mousetrap, because that's where the magic is. That's where your secret leverage lies.

But how do you master mastery by slowing down? How do you master time that way? Don't you fall behind?

No, because slowing down gets you in harmony. You're not out of tune any longer.

Without slowing down, you get way out ahead of life itself. I'm only asking you to slow down to the speed of life. You want to dance *with* life, not race out ahead of life.

People who race out ahead of life are falling down on the dance floor. They are living in their own future, which is where fear lives. But when you slow down to master this present moment, life gets fearless.

For example, I was coaching a man I will call Ben. Ben was excited because a large company had hired him to come in to give them a 60-minute talk. Ben couldn't wait. The talk was on his calendar for a month from now and he knew exactly what he was going to present. It was a talk he had given many times before and he knew it would be a big hit.

So now that it was all set and on his calendar, Ben was onto other things. Ben was spending his days racing around mentally and physically trying to get other new business. He was answering every call, checking email thirty times a day and living in a whirlwind of chaos. Ben was always in his own future, so Ben was always anxiety ridden (as all anxiety is about the future).

My job as Ben's coach was simply to *slow him down*. Down to the speed of life itself. Because life was on Ben's side; he just couldn't see it. He saw life as a giant opponent. Something that needed to be won over.

Once Ben relaxed and let himself take some deep breaths, I asked him to go back to the client who had hired him for a talk.

"What if someone passed a law," I said to Ben, "that said you could only have one client for the rest of your life and you would have to make all your income from this one client, and this was your client, Ben. What would you do?"

Ben was silent. I could see he was thinking.

I asked Ben to spend the rest our coaching session thinking about this one client. To slow everything down, as if this client were the only thing that existed in his world.

I was teaching Ben to go non-linear... to be a time warrior. The time warrior slows time to a standstill. Now there is no time. Ultimate victory. There is only timeless, eternal presence. Or "now."

Ben and I began to list the many other ways he would *love* to serve that company. He wrote a list of people in the company he wanted to go visit prior to his talk, to gather research on the many problems and challenges Ben could help them with. Two weeks later Ben had converted a $3,000 one-time speaking contract into a full year's program with more than twenty times that income.

Just by slowing down and applying what Bruce Lee talked about in the first quotation in this book: laser-like focus. That's the only difference between the average man and the warrior. The warrior has focus.

Remember that such focus cannot be frantic. It has to be relaxed and slowed down.

Notice when you're out on a boat and someone points out something on the shoreline for you to look at. If you strain your eyes, trying to force your focus, you won't see it. Only when you relax and let the image come to you do you now see it clearly.

Chapter 11

Let's all get drunk on information

We live in an embarrassment of information. We are connected to everything. It's all here. A few keystrokes away.

And the only downside is the intoxication of it. Because we can become drunk with options. Games, blogs, chats, videos, social media, gossip updates; there is no end to where we can go. Oh the places.

Two hours later we step back from the screen wondering where the two hours went. Sure, we took a lot in, but what went out?

That's why the warrior of time must keep his sword sharp and at the ready.

To carve out and cut away the clutter. To open up a clear space for creation. For it is active creation that will produce wealth and well-being. Not information.

Even though we understand the value of self-education, we know intuitively that we must, sooner or later, provide service to others. We must create something of value with our time.

Therefore, more than ever before, focus is vital. Uninterrupted time is the portal through which we now succeed. Not the flurry of multitasking and chaos.

And the addictive seduction of information is huge. It calls us. We may be alone, in silence and solitude, creating something powerful and new... and then: little dings and beeps and clicks from our devices call to us, like little tiny bartenders asking, "Can I pour you another?"

It's so easy to feel important and busy as we scurry like insects along linear time. One hour after another gets strung along. We are strung along and then we back away feeling strung out.

Our only hope is non-linear. It's certainly not in the old-fashioned time management tools. It's not the route of anally retentive linear organizing of task lists. But rather a rising up. A better use of this moment now, this eternal moment.

Pull something out of your future, and do it now.

Chapter 12

Okay, so, Why am I still procrastinating?

How do I distinguish between waiting (listening inside for inspiration) and procrastination?

(And really, while I'm at it, why do I need these labels, like "procrastination"? If I'm a passive, inert mass and I'm not in action, why do I need to label that? To find out if I'm procrastinating or not? Procrastination is a concept. Only.)

If I'm legitimately waiting for timing to be right and inspiration to emerge on a creative project, I have no problem waiting.

If I'm procrastinating (there is something to do that I know needs to be done) then I want to identify my next action.

And then I want to split the atom.

The atom is a very small thing, yet very powerful when split. The smallest acts are like atoms. They often turn out to be the most important acts of our lives. So once I identify the big scary imagined task as a distortion produced by my own worried mind, I want to go small, as small as possible.

What can I do in the next three minutes?

And when I say three minutes, that doesn't mean you can't take that smaller and split it from three to a minute and a half. Just do it.

Otherwise we (and I include myself) ruminate, brood, meditate and wander the intercranial halls of self-loathing and mental fatigue, making up all sorts of mystical stories that keep us fearful and passive. Dungeons, dragons and always out of action.

Chapter 13

Increase your capacity for living NOW

No valid plans for the future can be made
by those who have no capacity for living now.

Alan Watts

The time warrior steals from the future.

Then she pours her stolen gold—all of it—into the present moment. Like sand out of a boot into a sand painting. She pours from the future into the present. She embraces the present and increases her capacity for living. Only then can the future truly be bright.

When I coach people who have small businesses, or who are coaches or consultants, or who raise children or lead other people, I notice that their greatest opportunity for success is right in front of them in the very next conversation they are about to have.

Yet they fly past that conversation, barely tagging it like in a schoolyard game, racing to get to their "better" future.

When I recommend that they slow down it goes against their inner anxiety—the anxiety that runs their lives—as they strain so hard against their leash. The leash begins to choke them off and they start to lose oxygen. At night, they don't sleep, they just eventually pass out.

No wonder no valid plans for the future can be made. Those plans are all fear-based (invalid) because they want a "better" world than the one that presents itself in this next conversation, this world of infinite opportunity.

There is no way you can't have
the best business on this planet.
No one stops you but you…
that's the only possibility.

Byron Katie

Chapter 14

Now let's all stand up and stretch

No one stops me but me.

There was a time in my life when I didn't stretch much. I lived a life of fear. Fear is what I based my choices on.

Then I sobered up from my addictions and started life over. Then I got a coach who became my life coach and made sure I was always stretching. You can find out about him on www.theultimatecoach.net. He became my business coach, too. Soon I was stretching for the pure joy of stretching! Not to arrive anywhere in the future, but to actually arrive in the present moment. These words always remind me of the thrill of that stretch:

Sound when stretched is music.
Movement when stretched is dance.
Mind when stretched is meditation.
Life when stretched is celebration.

Shri Ravishankar Jee

Chapter 15

Replace knowing with choosing

If you are passive and don't go to war with your old, smothering, limited beliefs then time will ruin you. It will throw you around like a rag doll.

But the more you go to war the more liberated you become because this enemy called "time" retreats so fast. Then it surrenders to you. Soon there is no "time" to deal with. There is nothing to deal with but this wonderful opportunity at your door.

If you can walk you can dance. If you can talk you can sing. If you can shoo a coyote off your back porch you can be a warrior.

The coyote is anything that interrupts your devoted time.

And you don't have to know how to do it. Knowing takes time. Choosing, on the other hand, *makes* time. Just choose to do it.

Most people believe a deficit in *knowing* is their problem—which is why they have such a challenge with time. They believe they don't *know* what to do. So it will take time before they do it. They think they don't know "how to" do the thing that obviously needs to be done.

Learning "how to" takes lots and lots of time. Past, present and future time.

But choosing! Takes no time. When you choose you've already chosen. In the moment of the choice you have already chosen. It's already in the past. No time.

That's why I work with myself and my clients on the art of choosing. It frees us up to live more productively. It gets things done. Goals are reached. Work is accomplished. New levels of wealth and happiness are achieved. Choosing is non-linear time management and it is the way of the warrior.

My client Marta was a builder of websites and a consultant to online businesses. She wanted clients herself but she didn't know who to call. Notice that her problem was with "knowing." She didn't *know* who to call. That's why she was having such a hard time with time management.

So when I sat down to work with her we changed the focus from knowing to choosing.

We went through her computer and old emails and *chose* 20 people for her to call. Then, after her session with me she chose to make the calls. Those conversations led to more conversations and she began to report to me, via email, that she now had two, three and now four new clients.

Choosing is a power that is often overlooked for an entire professional lifetime. Until there is no choice left. Which is kind of a grim way to end life. On that clueless, powerless note.

Chapter 16

Failure is the ultimate success

I've missed more than 9,000 shots in my career. I've lost more than 300 games. Twenty-six times I've been trusted to take the game-winning shot, and missed. I've failed over and over and over again in my life... and that's why I succeed.

Michael Jordan

It really isn't fear of failure that stops us from trying exciting things. It's fear of the appearance of failure. It's the fear of looking like a failure.

Because if we fail in private, with no one knowing, it doesn't matter. If I try to write a poem in the privacy of my room and fail, who cares? If I try to do something that no one knows I tried to do, and I fail to do it, I don't mind that at all.

So the problem isn't really fear of failure, is it? It's fear of appearing to be a failure. So it's back to living my whole life for the sake of appearances, for the sake of other people liking me and approving of me.

Time warriors drop all of that. In fact, it's the FIRST THING they drop forever. They don't live for the approval of others. They live for the service project they are committed to.

Theory is good for the intellect,
but action is good for the soul.
It's also good for your mental
health, your physical health, and
your pocketbook.

Robert Ringer

Chapter 17

Warm up to what you're doing

Worry produces the opposite of action. It produces a chilly block of Jell-O where a human heart used to be. Trembling.

Therefore, worry is the ultimate in dysfunction. It's a misuse of the imagination. It chills the body.

But if you're a warrior, you want the body to be hot. Or at least warm. Warm and friendly until you catch even more enthusiasm for your task (which happens by doing it) and soon you are on fire.

Why keep doing the default into worry when it keeps you mentally spinning in your own worst-case future when you could have been taking action in the present moment? Notice again: Worry chills the body.

Action warms the body into fire.

The biggest fallacy there is about making good use of one's time is that you *have to feel like doing something* before you can do it. That you have to know how to *motivate yourself* prior to your action.

Try this: Have the action happen first. You can work up a sweat with wild action just by doing it. Then a funny thing happens. The motivation shows up. It was there all along.

The feel-like-it feeling was always there after all!

Plato was a philosopher, so most people just talk about his thoughts and theories as mental concepts. But Plato also said, "Lack of activity destroys the good condition of every human being, while movement and methodical physical exercise save it and preserve it."

Chapter 18

And the money will follow

I always heard the message, "Do what you love and the money will follow." In certain ways, that message has truth to it.

But it can also be confusing, and have us (like it did me) searching around endlessly for some perfect calling or purpose or job I'm always "better suited" for. Instead of just creatively working at whatever I am doing.

Now I've come to learn that this statement is more in line with reality for me: "Love what you do and the money will follow."

Now that works!

Even if you are doing a non-ideal job, if you do it with joy and creativity and great, surging, inappropriate energy, someone will promote you very fast. Soon you'll run the whole company. Because you are loving what you are doing. Nothing gets more attention than that.

Chapter 19

Should I just do the whole thing?

A lot of people ask me about the stories in *The Story of You* about people who simply assault the task they've been putting off. And yes sometimes I urge people to overwhelm their procrastinated task with massive action.

What about breaking it down to tiny sub-tasks? Isn't that a contradiction?

Well, you can do that, too! Because I do respect action. Both kinds. The kind that breaks a big job down into smaller actions and executes those actions as process goals and creates win after win after win until the big goal is reached. I do love that.

I also advocate the other way: a massive overwhelming of the entire challenge all at once. That's fun, too!

One approach does not exclude the other. There is more than one way to move a football down the field. Short passes. A draw play. Deep passes. All fun. And a lot depends on the score and the time left in the game.

What I do *not* advocate is being out of action. Waiting. Trying to decide things. Calling time out. Then calling another time out. Being frozen while making difficult decisions. I do not advocate that at all. It leads to misery.

Stop trying to decide what to do.

Just choose something and do it.

Chapter 20

Creating your future

The best way to predict the future is to create it.

Peter Drucker

People without creative mindsets lapse into the victim position without even realizing it.

Just like a garden does. Without nurturing care, a garden lapses into weeds and dying plants. Faded yellows and browns. The mind does that, too. Without nurturing, it lapses.

It goes to default mode of faded brown and yellow, ominous stories. It becomes a victim of circumstance.

And then the fear creeps in. On insect's feet. When you've lapsed into victim, fear creeps into every part of your life. Even the formerly beautiful parts that you used to feel so grateful for: Your family, friends and children. Fresh fears creep in about them. A person mentions your child's name and your heart stops. That once beautiful gift of a child is now something that causes your system to crash at the very thought of him.

Soon you look at family and friends and feel bad for what *might happen.* (See what the future does to you?) You fear for them and you fear for yourself should anything ever "happen."

The story of you is no longer inspiring. It's no longer a story you'd ever read a child at bedtime. If you wanted them to sleep peacefully.

And the fear doesn't stop there. Because you also fear poor health. And you fear your money will run out.

No wonder there is no more creativity available to you. There is no more love of life! To a victim mindset, love of life is now just a childhood memory.

But warriors clap their hands and turn that all around. Clap their hands and bring the light. They can get up *into* the light and dance and laugh and sing and feel action again. Any one of us can do that.

The great warrior who invented Aikido said this:

In the art of peace a single cut of the sword
links past, present and future; it absorbs the universe.
Time and space disappear.

Morihei Ueshiba

Chapter 21

Serving is the opposite of pleasing

The most efficient usc of your time is to serve with it. Serving is always effective. It always has an amazing (though sometimes delayed) return on investment of energy.

The least efficient use of your time is to please people with it. To try to win approval. To impress someone.

Most people who feel stuck are devoting their days to trying to figure out what other people could be thinking of them. It's an endless, fruitless, hopeless task of rolling a "pander" stone up a hill, fighting to win the acceptance and love of others.

Besides that, even successful pleasing never lasts. (Small, annoying detail.)

Because you wake up the next morning in a cold sweat, trusting no one to remember how you won them over. So it has to start all over.

Ineffective people think they need more and more love from others. They go to their counselors, mentors, coaches, therapists, religious guides and they ask, HOW DO I GET MORE LOVE COMING MY WAY?

Here is what they never ask: "How can I love more than I am now loving?"

If that were their inquiry, time, love and money would not be a problem.

Chapter 22

More ways to kiss the ground

*Today, like every other day, we wake up empty
and frightened. Don't open the door to the study
and begin reading. Take down a musical instrument.
Let the beauty we love be what we do.
There are hundreds of ways to kneel and kiss the ground.*

Rumi

Learn to be fearless in some areas of your life, and then let the joy spread.

Work the areas where you are not yet fearless, and bring love in. Bring a ruthless warrior's sword of inquiry into the belief system that keeps you in fear.

Fear is like darkness.

Darkness isn't anything. It is the absence of light. Light is something! But darkness is nothing at all. You can bring the light, and there is no more darkness.

In just the same way, fear is merely the absence of love. If you can bring enough love, there is no more fear.

If you desired to change the world, where would you start? With yourself or others?

Alexander Solzhenitsyn

Chapter 23

The way of inspiration

Maybe I'm fine now. Maybe I'm already an inspired time warrior, living from my spirit instead of circumstance.

Maybe I should go out and evangelize and help others to be like me!

Hold on.

There is only one person I can ever really ultimately work on, and that is me. Forgetting that fact can be tragic. Or, at the very least, quite painful.

The fastest way to convert someone from being a victim to being a warrior is through inspiration. People being inspired by your demonstration of *what happened when I worked on me.* People being inspired spontaneously, of their own accord, from inside themselves.

Victims and pessimists hate to be fixed, hate to be corrected, and even hate to be taught things. Because their whole position is defensive.

Whenever I tell a victim, "Well, you know you are kind of a victim—you are very pessimistic about this," they become extremely defensive and try to reinforce their position so that it becomes a deeply justified position. My remark has backfired on me.

If my intention is to help someone become a happier person and have a bigger outlook, I want to make sure I don't produce the opposite of that by judging them. I don't want to push them deeper into their own pessimism by trying to fix them.

And so many people make this mistake. They criticize their teenage son for being moody and pessimistic and it only drives that poor boy deeper into himself. All he can hear is "There's something wrong with you, I don't approve of you, and I don't understand you." Now there is even greater alienation.

So all this fixing, correcting, improving and criticizing does not work with people. Therefore it qualifies as a waste of time, which is the very subject of this book, no?

The fastest, best way to connect with others is through something called inspiration.

I want to ask: Have I become an inspirational figure in this person's life? That would be the warrior's inquiry, because no other way will work.

If I'm not an inspirational figure in the lives of the pessimists around me they will not convert to optimism through me. They may still convert to optimism through *something*. It could be through some inspiring event or some inspiring person or some inspiring situation, or even an inspiring book can get it going.

But it won't be through me.

Religions are started not just by what a person teaches but by who that person is *being*. The inner glow. The magnetic, inspiring example that person sets. The feeling people get when they are by his or her side.

The teaching part might come later. *Being* always comes first.

Now look back on your own life. All the major changes you have made that have moved you toward the light—toward greater creativity, toward more fearless action, toward things that you enjoy. Look, too, at what has called you toward more maturity and effectiveness.

Hasn't it always begun with inspiration?

Has it ever occurred through somebody criticizing you, fixing you, making you wrong and hurting your feelings and making you defensive? That is not a route to change. It will not change another person.

Chapter 24

Try risking your identity

You have to be able to risk your identity
for a bigger future than the present you are living.

Fernando Flores

That's it, right there.

Right in the quote by Fernando Flores. That's what has to happen for an individual to go from pretty okay to absolutely great—at whatever endeavor. A person must *lose* that freaking identity because it's his worst enemy.

Be *who you need to be* in the moment. And then be willing to change that in a heartbeat.

Just as the samurai would die before going into battle, you will want to do the same: die to who you are. Let your cherished, built-up personality pass away.

This ego, this personality, this identity was finished being made up for most people in junior high school. Therefore it's just full of adolescent fear, worry and anxious hope.

Let's start with hope. Here is the problem with hope: Hope is always producing a longing... a longing for external circumstances to change while ignoring the beautiful internal resources already there.

Another quote from Flores that might apply here is: "Hope is the raw material of losers."

What exactly am I hoping for, and why?

Someone to watch over me? Some change of fortune?

My ego dreams of external things and then it hopes and fears it won't get them. How is that effective? My ego identity is almost entirely made up of dreams, hopes and fears. Why do I want to come from there?

Hope is why I can spend days without making a single creative move... not one single inspired communication... not even a *chance* for a beautiful gesture.

Hope and fear. Interchangeable. Unsustainable.

Here's what my friend Ken Wilber says about this ego of ours that we use for an identity:

"If we are going to insist on identifying with just the little self in here, then others are going to bruise it, insult it, injure it. The ego, then, is kept in existence by a collection of emotional insults; it carries its personal bruises as the fabric of its very existence. It actively collects hurts and insults, even while resenting them, because without its bruises it would be, literally, nothing."

Chapter 25

Notice I am saying warrior, not worrier

The worried mind wakes up in the morning and projects worst-case scenarios into the future. That's what it thinks its job is.

And, as it has been proven—to the chagrin of pharmaceutical companies whose new drugs have to perform "against placebo" and often don't—the placebo effect (the effect of believed thoughts on the body) is really, really real.

Really.

Thoughts of fear, dread and the worst future I can picture have me ready to not act. Or, as executive coach Dusan Djukich told a room full of people recently, when he was asked *what should we do when we are afraid:* "Take DECISIVE ACTION and your fear won't matter. Take that decisive action enough times and your fear won't exist any more."

Chapter 26

Asking the wrong question

The question isn't, Who is going to let me;
it's Who is going to stop me?

Ayn Rand

I love this question Ayn Rand prefers. Because for most of my life I was asking the other question: Who is going to let me?

I was looking outside myself for permission and approval all day. A very nasty habit that leads to poverty and broken relationships.

But a habit all the same. A habit almost every single one of us acquires in childhood. The quest for permission and approval. It's how childhood is run. It's how we are domesticated so that we aren't just running with the wolves.

But it's a habit that does not serve the grown up mature adult at all. In fact, it is the very habit that eventually eats away at the spirit of the grown person.

When my songwriting partner Fred Knipe and I wrote a song called "I Can't Get To You From Here," we of course never knew if anyone outside of our families would ever hear it. We created the song anyway. We didn't think about the approval of others, because that would have stopped the creation of the song.

Now more than 70,000 people have watched the YouTube version of the song, which you can see here: www.youtube.com/watch?v=AzrljQ0Euto

It wasn't a matter of "Who's going to let us?" write songs for a living. It was a matter of "Who's going to stop us?"

Chapter 27

Another way to see yourself

I gave a seminar recently that identified two kinds of people in the world: creators and reactors.

I love doing these either/or kinds of teachings because people remember the contrasts forever. If you make a clear either/or distinction, people can immediately access that, and see life from one side or the other.

They can also choose to quickly jump over the divide from one to the other.

If seminars simply give out lots of information, they will not be transformative. I've learned that from experience. In fact an "informative" seminar will bog people down with a lot of things to try to remember.

One top leader called me once and asked "What kind of information?" was in my creators/reactors talks and I said there was none.

"No information?" he said.

"No, just a single distinction that gets repeated and illustrated throughout the seminar so people can use it and never forget it."

He said, "I'd have to have you give me a list of bullet points of the information in your talk before I could get my company to hire you for our keynote this fall."

"There aren't any bullet points," I said.

"I don't know how you expect to be hired," he said, "Or how you expect to be booked."

"I don't expect anything," I said. "…in any area of my life."

"Then how do you make your living?"

"By speaking to groups unlike yours who are led by people unlike you."

He later decided to hire me. Even though it was clear I had a significant personality problem. (I've never denied that.)

Creators create their day based on a compelling, irresistible future. Reactors are reacting to the opinions of others all day.

Creators are always to be found in the middle of another bold creative move while reactors are on the phone reporting another travesty or injustice they have just suffered.

Creators create their futures by what they do today. Reactors are obsessed with talking about the immediate unfortunate past. The best future a reactor ever produced was simply a bandaged-up version of the past. For them, a fresh, new future is never created. Therefore, for them, life is always unfair.

I was one of them. A reactor. Big time. I was sick, ruined, bankrupt, addicted to drugs and alcohol, lying to everyone I knew, especially the ones closest to me. A life of fear and more fear. The best I could ever feel, on my best day, was just worried. I was often okay with being worried. It was better than being flat-out terrified. But the terror would always return. And the pink cloud period of constant worry never lasted.

My life was saved by a recovery program.

Then, from there, I had the stunning privilege of learning to live freely. I never knew how before. Now I found teachers. I found new books. I found friends who were learning the same thing. I found a mentor.

I found creativity.

I work with people now who are learning to create their own futures. I coach them. People call it life coaching, and that's just a handy term. Who knows what really happens when two people work with each other to create a good, prosperous life?

If I was born in the image of my Creator then I know what my job is: to create. It's that simple.

If, on the other hand, I was born in the image of my Destroyer, then my job is to react. To figure out how to please people and react to everything they say to me. To worry constantly about how to win their approval.

Until the worrying finally, totally, destroys *me*.

That's when I want to talk to my Destroyer. "Why," I ask him desperately, "are you leading me down this obsequious path of constant people-flattering? Why am I on this quest for total approval? Because the more approval I try to win, the worse I feel."

What I got in my spiritual recovery was that winning the approval of other people is a descent into cowardice as a man. It's the act of going pathetic in the face of circumstance. Surrendering my own power to the judgment of my superiors, who would be just about everybody. Such activity had me despising myself and resenting others.

So how can winning friends and influencing people be the good mission everybody says it is?

Chapter 28

Want to know who you are?

Do you want to know who you are? Don't ask. Act!
Action will delineate and define you.

Thomas Jefferson

I can spend the whole day in a deep soft chair trying to decide who I really am, trying to decide what to do next, trying to decide why I do what I do, trying to decide all kinds of things.

But I notice that I am now less effective and capable as a human, and my sense of trust in myself is disappearing. I call this Decision Misery. I used to be there a lot. It's a flat, linear place.

Then I learned about something called action.

I learned I can solve all this worry and decision-making anxiety by taking action. By admiring action. By having action plans, by asking, whenever stuck, WHAT'S MY NEXT ACTION? And then, doing that action NOW. Action. Movement. Decisive energy. Solves most everything!

Chapter 29

How do I make her perfect?

The paradox of change in others is this. People change faster when they don't need to. People change faster when they're already perfect the way they are.

So if I'm sitting with you and in my eyes and in my heart you're just perfect the way you are, you now feel more freedom to change. You now have a sense of safety and peace and openness.

If your wife walks in and says, "I think I'm going to go on a diet," and you say, "Thank goodness!" that's not very supportive, even though you think it is. It's not supportive because she is embarrassed by your urgent agreement that she "needs" to change.

The best thing you can say when she says she's going on a diet is, "Why?"

"Well, don't you think I should lose some weight?"

"No, I think you're perfect the way you are. I don't have any opinion on that. That's your business, your world, it's your life. I'm fine with you. You're the perfect you for me."

"Well, OK. But don't you think I should lose weight?"

"Not if you don't want to."

"Well, I do want to."

"I want what you want."

"Will you support me? Will you help me? Will you help me fix the meals I'm going to be eating on this program?"

"Of course."

"Because you think I should lose weight, don't you?"

"No. It's just the project you're on. If you love it, I'm into it."

"All right then."

If someone is perfect the way they are, they have freedom now to create a new path without feeling judged or feeling they *need to.*

Without feeling they have to. Without feeling they "should." Because all those negative beliefs of obligation will have it not happen.

That's the basic rebellion of a free human being.

Thinking you are obligated or thinking you *have to* will have you resist it and fight against it. But thinking it would be cool, and thinking it would be fun and thinking you would love it—now you are talking. Now you're really moving.

I want to *live* the optimism that tells me my loved ones are perfect the way they are. Because that saves me huge amounts of time. Can you even estimate the amount of time we waste judging others and worrying about them? What if that time were returned to us?

And when I say I want to *live* this optimism about others, I am differentiating that from preaching it. So many people make that mistake. "I try to tell my children... I've always tried to teach them how to... I try to get them to be more..."

Wait a minute. Let them *see it* for themselves.

Chapter 30

Capture the problem

Time management is actually just problem management, isn't it?

When a problem comes up, what do you do? If you are a time warrior, you capture the problem. Straight away.

In other words, you write it down. You take it away from the emotional realm. Once it's on paper, it sits there as a neutral object, just like a crossword puzzle sits there for your amusement. You know the minute you write it down that solving things can now become amusing and entertaining.

Writing it down has removed the problem from the ephemeral emotional realm of "something horrible." You've eliminated the sense of doom.

Now that it's written down it's going to go somewhere. Maybe you'll take it in to your coaching session with your coach. Maybe you'll take it out with you for a long walk. You might have it go into a phone call you make.

Once you've captured it and written it down, it no longer lives in the back of your mind.

The former enemy is now in captivity. And he's ready to talk.

You know that feeling whenever a problem is lingering back in your mind. You know it's there. You can feel it back there. You're walking around, trying to live, trying to communicate about other things, trying to have relationships but you've always got this feeling in the back of your mind. Like a mood parasite.

It produces a gloomy tone, almost like a bass cello playing behind you, playing low notes in a minor key and you're feeling like something's wrong, something's not right, something's not complete. There is unfinished business and that will always stand between you and whatever you're doing. You won't do what you're doing in a fully self-expressive way when you have this problem and it isn't being managed. It isn't being captured, it hasn't been put down.

So step one is to capture your problem and write it down.

Notice the free, powerful feeling that already gives you and you haven't even solved the problem yet!

Chapter 31

Redefine the problem

The second warrior step in rapid problem-solving is to redefine the problem. In other words, I no longer want it to be a "problem."

And I don't mean just glossing it over with a phony new "positive" word. I mean really, truly converting this thing (whatever it is) from a problem in my mind into something entirely different.

How about calling it a project?

A project is a lot more fun, emotionally. A person can have a favorite project. A person will never have a favorite problem.

Words carry emotional histories. When people have "projects," they can wake up excited about doing their projects. They know that when they finish their projects, they'll get a good feeling—a sense of completion, a sense of accomplishment!

We are glad to have projects in front of us that we can work on today, because we derive self-esteem and a sense of accomplishment from finishing projects. Wrapping them up, putting them to bed, knowing they are done, taken care of and handled.

You may have noticed that in our society we reserve the word "problem" for the worst, most troubling kinds of things. Somebody walks home and they have been listening to the radio and they say:

"Hey, have you heard about Tiger Woods?"

"What?"

"He's got real problems."

"Oh, my gosh"

"His golf career is threatened by real problems now."

And so "problems" is the word we use when people encounter the most dire, horrible circumstances. Therefore I don't want problems in my mind. I want projects.

Even though the secret truth about problems is that problems are actually good for us.

Let's say your child is in math class and you go in at the start of the year and it's open house and the parents are meeting the teacher and the teacher says to you, "We're going to give your boy more problems to solve this year than last year's class had. We've got it set up so this year's children will be working a lot more math problems and solving twice as many problems before the year is over. We're able to do this because of the computer system we now have and some new teaching methods. Your child will emerge as being much better (more masterful) than last year's or any previous class because of this new problems-enhanced program we have."

Now if you are a parent you are thinking "Hey, that's terrific. I love that. That sounds great. Did you hear that, Hon? Our kid's going to have more problems to solve."

We secretly know that problems strengthen people. They are good for people, not bad. (Especially when someone else is the one solving the problems. Then we see it clearly.) Problems actually build skill levels up. Problems turn people into more self-confident people.

But when we ourselves have a problem show up we tremble and hide.

So redefining the problem is a really important step. Problems are good for us but we don't really know that because of the emotional baggage we've attached to the *word* "problem."

A time warrior's life is filled with new projects.

Chapter 32

For goodness sake get some help!

Now you've got a project. Good.

But if your project looks too big to do quickly, go to someone. Sit down with someone. If you have a coach, sit down with your coach. Take the problem that you've written out and put it in front of your coach and make sure you *both* look at it.

The reason coaches are so good at working with people is because they don't have the emotional charge on a client's problem that the client has. When the client thinks, "This shouldn't be happening to me," the client is now disempowered by his own emotions.

The coach, a consultant, or anybody who can sit with you and look at the problem with you, is *not* going to bring any emotional baggage to this problem. They will have a healthy distance from the problem. (They are going to be actually higher than a kite looking at this problem because it's not their problem and they love solving clients' problems.) To them, it's just an intellectual challenge. It's like the Sunday crossword puzzle or a great mystery on TV they are watching and really enjoying trying to solve.

We human beings love trying to solve things. As long as they're not *our* things. The real trouble comes in when we think these things we are trying to solve *shouldn't be* in *our* lives, that they are bad for us. That's when the real trouble comes in. Because then we slip down the ladder of consciousness (and resourcefulness) to very low levels. It affects our creative ability and our clarity of thought. Our cognitive power is diminished. We struggle. We avoid. We try to escape. We procrastinate. Soon we even think it's a time management problem! It's not. It's an emotional problem.

Most "time management" problems actually began as emotional problems.

It's really an exciting thing when I work with another person on my problem because pretty soon there are a lot more options available than I ever thought possible looking at this thing by myself.

Chapter 33

Honor something called completion

Now we get to the next step in the warrior's way to deal with problems. This is the most important step. This is the one you always want to make sure you do. This is the step in problem-solving that most people really don't want to do. But that, in itself, creates new problems!

The name of this step is **"complete."**

What you want to do with every project is to complete it. If you only solve part of it you'll still carry it around as unfinished business. Believe me, I know what I'm talking about. I'm not just whistling Dixie. I'm not just talking about clients that I've had that I've helped, I'm talking about my own life.

One of the last pieces of life's puzzle for me was to see the value in **completing** things.

Put it this way: A time warrior finishes things off. He finishes strong. Always. He has the killer instinct.

Notice how much energy it takes away to have unfinished business in life. How much that drains you.

In fact, it takes more energy to carry around unfinished business than it does to complete everything on your list—a lot more! Try it someday. Try waking up and pretending you're a robot or pretending you're Superman, or someone without feelings, just someone who can do things without considering whether they *feel like* doing them. Then do everything you can think of that's unfinished; and notice at the end of that day how much energy you've got. You'll be amazed. The more things you complete, the more energy you'll have.

That's a real paradox! When you finish something and complete it and tie a ribbon around it so that now it's done, your sense of energy about life goes *up*—it doesn't go down. You are exuberant after completion. It really feels great.

Notice at the end of a football game the team that wins is jumping all over the field. I mean, where do they get the energy? They have just been playing their hearts out all night long and here they are leaping and jumping into each other's arms and running in circles and running around on the field. Now they run around and extend their hands to the fans leaning over the railings from the stands! Look at the energy in these people. Now they go into the locker room and they're yelling and whooping and hollering and singing and dancing. Then they go out and party all night long. The sun is coming up and they are still partying. They still don't want to go to bed.

That's because a victory on the field makes them feel gloriously *complete*. They completed what they set out to do! There's no unfinished business.

Now notice the team on the *other* side of the field. They're just wiped out. They need help to get to the locker room. They're completely exhausted. They go home and they go straight to bed. They mope around for days. No energy. The reason they're wiped out is that it feels so *unfinished*.

So notice at the end of your day how the things that are *incomplete* will leave you feeling tired.

From now on cross off every task on your to-do list. Don't just half-finish it. Don't just finish the important part and leave a few things hanging out there. Finish the whole thing and tie a ribbon around it.

You might even call someone you're working for and ask, "Are we complete?" And if they say, "Yes, we're complete," notice how you feel. There's a surge of energy.

I have a lot of people tell me, "I have a problem with procrastination. I put things off." The main reason people have a problem with procrastination is that they don't see the connection between completing something and having new, fresh energy come out of that. They actually imagine that working on this thing and finishing it would drain *even more* of their energy and they get tired just thinking about it, so they don't complete it.

They procrastinate because they already feel out of energy. They think, "I'm just not up for that. I don't have the heart. I don't have the will to finish that task right now. I need sleep. I need to start fresh tomorrow. I don't have the energy." But what they don't have is completion.

They just don't see it.

They don't see that leaving things unfinished is what's causing the low levels of energy. So procrastination causes procrastination! The more you procrastinate, the less energy you have.

You would think it's the other way around. Most of us believe (believe me—I believed it for years) the more things I leave unfinished, the more energy I'm "preserving" for the really important things that might come up.

Not true.

It's the opposite. The more things I finish and know are complete and I can cross off my list, the more I can say to myself, "I'm totally, fully, complete with that," the more *whole* I feel as a human being.

Procrastinators are very worried about things. Soon they don't have much of a mind left. Because their mind has been eaten up by these parasites called unfinished tasks.

The final warrior step in solving problems is to make certain you are complete.

Chapter 34

I'm depressed by other people's suffering

Feeling depressed is not a good place to begin. It's not a good use of your time. If you are wanting to help others, you will not want to cultivate that feeling.

Wherever conditions are bad, in Tibet or Haiti, or the inner city, it does not help to think that "compassion" requires that you actually feel their pain and be dragged into depression by it.

The problem is not located in Haiti or Tibet, but in the human mind. Because since the beginning of time there has always been a situation like Haiti.

The warrior's question is *what can we do about it?* George Clooney saw the Haiti situation and got busy, sprung into action, and organized a huge telethon for Haiti. He worked day and night, and his energy was high. He was really helping.

Others just got depressed.

Opportunities to help others are exciting unless we twist them in our minds and brood about them and then start to add all the depressing language to the situation like "unfair" and "suffering" and all that. That pulls us down into gloom and worry and despair and we can no longer help.

Happy people are a bigger help to others than worried people.

Which is why a medic on the battlefield, to be really good at what she does, feels no negative feelings about the dead and wounded, but just cranks up the adrenaline and *helps*.

Doctors in Haiti right now who are laughing, joking with the children, keeping their staff's spirits high, are a bigger help than the doctors weeping in front of the cameras for CNN. The weeping doctors thought Haiti was all about *them* and their own feelings. All that weeping takes energy away from what they could be doing to really help someone. Hey Doc. It's not about you. It's about the kids. Get busy. Tell the media to buzz off.

Happy people help more people than "concerned," "caring," "sensitive" people who over-emphasize "feeling empathy" instead of actually rolling up their sleeves, getting their hands dirty and helping.

An overly empathetic person creates a poor relationship with time and energy. A time warrior does not ask, "How do I feel?" but rather asks, "How can I help?"

Chapter 35

What are people yearning for?

What people *think* they are yearning for is to have the externals in their lives change: other people, outside circumstances, cash flow, romance, behavior of children, you name it.

However, what they discover if they look deep enough is that outside change makes no inside change. Everything still feels the same. (Notice the study of lottery winners that prove that millions of dollars do not change their feelings at all.) No matter how circumstances change, it's the inside that stays the same. (The inside is the *kingdom within* I experience as the real, true me.)

When I can shift my yearning from the outside to myself, then I can start becoming fulfilled. Happiness grows from the inside out. Outside circumstance has nothing to do with happiness and that's an insight most people never have.

Chapter 36

Making good use of hard times

Sometimes hard times and recessions can return us to the principles we always wanted to live by anyway. The principles that give us pride and satisfaction. Like this one: A penny saved is a penny earned. Or, self-reliance. (As a startling new concept.) And even this: One hour of planning saves three days of confusion.

Then, when the "hard times" lift, as they always do, we are stronger and wiser. So my question to myself is not "How Will I Survive This?" It's "How Will I Use This?"

Hard economic times are bad for us. Is that true? Whenever I have anything at all in my life that appears "bad" for me I pull out my Byron Katie books and CDs and plunge back into her Work. I recommend her to you as well. Don't just frequent her writings but do the difficult and courageous Work she invites you to do and really do it. Follow the simple directions. Don't just sit on the edge of the water and put your toe in the water, but jump in and swim, and swim. It will take more courage than you ever thought you had to challenge those thoughts.

If you read Victor Frankl's account of life inside a Nazi prison camp (*Man's Search for Meaning*), you will be convinced that external circumstances and "hard times" really mean nothing compared to the spirit that is yours to grow.

We can all get caught up in the upheaval of our banking systems, real estate, credit cards, and really scare ourselves. But what would you like to create today?

Ralph Waldo Emerson said, "A political victory, a rise of rents, the recovery of your sick, the return of your absent friend, or some other favorable event raises your spirits, and you think good days are preparing for you. Do not believe it. Nothing can bring you peace but yourself. Nothing can bring you peace but the triumph of principles."

Chapter 37

Go to war against distraction

Jonathan Franzen is now thought by most literary critics to be the greatest living American novelist. His book, *The Corrections* sold many millions of copies and nine years later he has emerged with another complex bestseller, *Freedom*.

Lev Grossman wrote an interesting profile of Franzen for Time Magazine when the new novel came out, and as I was reading it I realized that Franzen was a time warrior. (It might have something to do with his greatness.)

Grossman described Franzen's writing life, which begins at 7 a.m. and is stripped of all distractions. He works in a rented office that has nothing in it but a single computer. "He uses a heavy, obsolete Dell laptop from which he has scoured any trace of hearts and solitaire, down to the level of the operating system," writes Grossman. "Because Franzen believes you can't write serious fiction on a computer that's connected to the Internet, he not only removed the Dell's wireless card, but also permanently blocked its Ethernet port. 'What you have to do,' he explains, 'is you plug in an Ethernet cable with superglue, and then you saw off the little head of it.'"

How many little heads do *we* saw off in our own war against distraction? How many spartan disciplines do we introduce that counter today's information attacks that keep us distracted from our missions?

The warrior's war is against distraction.

Chapter 38

We know what we need to know

All of us know much more than we think we know. We may not know everything, but all of us have the chief resources we need to solve our problems.

Nathaniel Branden

The great author and psychologist Nathaniel Branden has helped countless people find the resources they have inside themselves to solve their problems. Fortunately, back in the late 1980s, I was a client of his and benefited greatly from his psychotherapy sessions.

Was I crazy enough back then to need psychotherapy? Oh my. Why did I wait so long? That was the real question.

Dr. Branden taught me to ask myself questions. Is the act I'm about to do going to raise or lower my self-esteem? Is the day I am planning out going to end up raising my self-esteem or lowering it? It's a valuable guideline, and Dr. Branden's books are the best on this subject.

I used to wander the earth wondering what I "should" do and how I should do it. I'd look outside myself for all the answers.

But the answers were inside me all along. I always knew much more than I thought I knew. I always had all the resources I ever needed to solve my problems in life.

And so do all the people I know today. They've got all they need. There is a creative spirit inside each one of them, ready to self-express and find the next action.

Chapter 39

What do victims do?

Victims think of a lot of things they "should" be doing to improve their lives, but then they think they are just too busy to do them now. They are soon focused on their troubles.

Warriors focus on the next quantum leap of success. (In life, what you focus on grows.)

The time warrior does surprisingly good things NOW. His ruthless sword cuts through all the nonsense of impressing people and leaves only love and service in its wake.

And now is when it all happens. And if it can't literally happen now, the warrior sets precise deadlines. Sets them up now. He sets the deadlines NOW, so that they are still in the NOW. Deadlines soon become the warrior's best friend: "We're changing our price structure January 1st, we are hiring our new marketing director by March 15th, we are going to have the house painted and made over by April 30th and we will have the whole neighborhood papered with our new flier by noon Friday."

The human brain is a magical bio-computer. It sends us energy when we send it something clearly inspiring. But it drags us way down when we feed it something that is negative or depressing. The key to all of this is that *we* send it.

WE SEND IT.

Life itself doesn't send the brain anything. Family members don't. The news on TV doesn't. We do. Only we have that access to the brain.

("This recession is waking us up, making us more honest and stronger," versus "This recession is getting me down." Both are chosen messages. One sends energy and enthusiasm, the other sends sadness and fatigue.)

Again. The brain sends the body energy when we send the brain something inspiring.

It's a biology lesson the time warrior never forgets.

Chapter 40

Do you fear death or commitment?

When you say you fear death you are really saying
that you fear you have not lived your true life.
This fear cloaks the world in silent suffering.

David Viscott

The breakdown of language foretells the breakdown of results. Always.

For example, when I say I was committed to doing X but I only did Y, I have misused the word commitment, and language no longer means anything.

So now anything I say is just noise that conveys no power at all.

My language can no longer make anything happen. It can still be descriptive (it can tell you how I feel, it can describe the past) but it can no longer be generative (it can't make things happen).

First of all, a commitment is something you keep, no matter what. It's not something that feels optional to you. For example, you have a commitment that your kids won't go hungry. No matter what happens, you lose your job, whatever, and you still keep that commitment. Because your kids are important to you? No. Because it's a commitment.

I had a friend who kept breaking promises and then saying he was sorry and it was not what he was committed to doing. I finally told him that he misunderstood commitment, because commitments, by definition, are kept. He said, "Ontologically speaking I've related to commitments as who I am and not something I have."

That's exactly where he checked out of the game. Commitments are not something ontological or theoretical. They are creations. You make them up. Then you keep them. You have total control of them.

He had said to me in many communications that things he was "committed to" simply didn't happen. I said to him, "Please realize (for your own sake so life is not such a frightening "mess" as you call it) that those were not commitments at all. They were intentions. Hoped-for outcomes, but certainly not anything you were committed to."

Some human beings have no commitments at all, and some have very few beyond the commitment to stay alive and out of jail. You can choose and make your commitments very carefully because you know that if they are commitments, you will keep them.

My same friend asked me, "Couldn't there be competing commitments in our committed place and commitments that are hidden from our view inside there? Like I may be committed to watching TV instead of committed to spending time with my family?"

How could you think of watching TV as a commitment? It could be an intention, or a choice for an activity. But a commitment is a really big deal. Maybe you promised your client you would watch her being interviewed on TV at 10 p.m. THAT is a commitment. But just to watch TV at the end of the day? There's no commitment in that.

What about "competing commitments"?

Don't make them. Why would I commit to finishing a work project and taking my kids to the zoo on the same Saturday if the commitments compete? I would not do that.

Commitments are things you keep no matter what happens to make them difficult to keep. Commitments are powerful. So be very selective when using them.

Just like a flame-thrower is a powerful weapon. It's not necessary to own one, but it makes an intruder think twice before proceeding further into your home when you show him what it can do.

Commitments are like that.

Chapter 41

The past as a regrettable thing

I used to have creative ideas, and then never put them into practice, and then I'd label myself with negative words and judgments.

Today I don't place a lot of value in regretting my past or even trying to understand it. Identifying past patterns and labeling my flaws and weaknesses. Not much value in that because the present moment opportunity disappears while I do that.

How do I want to be *now*? Do I want to finish what I start? I can do that. But I just have to do it. Which is me going on the offensive. Because the best defense is a great offense.

If someone is peppering my home with envelopes (past due bills) I can always make a game of this and take it down the field and pepper *their* goal with envelopes! Now it's fun. I'm on the offensive.

I once totally confused and destroyed the mentality of a major creditor of mine by sending them a check every day! It had them back on their heels playing defense every day, processing my relentless, *relentless* flurry of checks... Finally they were paid off.

So take it to them. Go on OFFENSE. Do not play defense with a creditor or you will lose the game element. You want to really be effective with your time? Get a game going.

Chapter 42

Good robot or bad robot?

My experience is that the only way for a warrior mind shift to work is for me to create (daily) an entirely fresh future for myself, and commit to living it now. Each day my commitment must be refreshed, renewed and rebooted; it won't "stick" on its own until it is.

That's when bad robotics transform into good robotics.

And I use the term "robot" to remind me that I have a higher self. When I'm at my best, keeping my life in good perspective, I am controlling a lower self, the bad robot. If I think that lower self is not a robot but rather a caring, feeling, "real me" person, my life is then run by confusing, ego-based emotions.

So I must transform how the world I wake up into looks to me.

I want to remember that I control both robots. I always have. And only the higher, wiser "good" robot is really me. Which makes it fun and allows me to not (ever) take setbacks personally.

You can do this, too. You can rise up and see how your bad robot is behaving and change it.

It's all a creation anyway, so why not make up the perceptions that get you the prosperous life you've always wanted but have not yet committed to?

I'm behind you all the way.

Chapter 43

Forget about your safety!

Most dysfunctional people are only trying to stay safe.

Most of your own lack of success comes from an exaggerated inner compulsion to feel safe and sound.

This changes when you stop living in the land of vague dreams and hopes and wishes. Dreams turn to nightmares, as well they should. The nightmare's function is to cure you of being a child and grow you up.

But the passive loser still just dreams. Even after the nightmare. While the time warrior wakes up from the nightmare, plans and executes a new life.

I love the quote at the bottom of Maurice Bassett's emails from Goethe that says, "Live dangerously and you live right."

My friend Michael Weitz sent this to me recently, and it is saying the same thing:

> *Forget safety.*
> *Live where you fear to live.*
> *Destroy your reputation.*
> *Be notorious.*
> **Rumi**

In the courses I teach companies on creating better relationships with internal and external customers, I take a long time studying the brilliant psychiatrist David Viscott's concepts of risking, and how important it is to be willing to risk throughout the day: risk loss of face and loss of ego, risk embarrassment in the name of creating and connecting and truly making a difference in someone else's life.

Dr. Viscott says:

"If you cannot risk, you cannot grow.
If you cannot grow, you cannot become your best.
If you cannot become your best, you cannot be happy.
And if you cannot be happy, what else matters?"

You can see how he weaves a direct link between risking and happiness itself. Our greatest growth spurts happen when we are children risking and daring and falling down and embarrassing ourselves.

Later, as adults, we find habits, addictions and comfort zones to hide out in, not even knowing we are doing it until we are on our deathbeds looking back.

Kicking ourselves.

For not living dangerously.

For not taking more risks. I picture a nursing home or a hospice in my future:

"Nurse! What's that loud noise in room 320?"

"Oh it's that old man Chandler kicking himself."

Chapter 44

Purpose transitions you

People can transition, or they can stay stuck at whatever level of sleep they've put themselves into. That's my experience of myself and everyone I've known.

A while back I was in Phoenix's Sky Harbor airport getting ready to fly to Portland to work with clients up there and I happened upon Jim Manton in the airport where he was getting ready to fly to Ohio. I was happy to see Jim, a great friend and wonderful business consultant. People get stuck, and Jim helps them transition.

He is a master coach who is humble about his own major past accomplishments as an executive with booming companies. The beauty of Jim is that he has kept transitioning himself.

As he says in his powerful book, *The Secret of Transitions*:

"To transition we must enter a state in which we are no longer what we once were, and yet we are not who we must become. We have to be willing to stand in the open gap and momentarily risk being nothing."

The biggest transitions I've ever seen occur happen when people stop associating fear with money, when people stop associating money with "self worth," and when people take up arms against scarcity and win the wealth battle (it's internal) once and for all. There are a hundred ways to do this, but most people never do any of them.

And speaking of taking up arms against scarcity, why is it that suicide rates go down during times of war? And suicide rates go up during times of financial crisis? This is a most important question to answer.

Nassim Nicholas Taleb was a trader on Wall Street during the big crash of 1987. He writes, "People on the sidewalk looked dazed. Earlier I had seen a few adults silently sobbing in the trading room of First Boston. I had spent the day at the epicenter of the events, with shell-shocked people running around like rabbits in front of headlights. When I got home, my cousin Alexis called to tell me that his neighbor committed suicide, jumping from his upper-floor apartment. It did not even feel eerie. It felt like Lebanon, with a twist: having seen both I was struck that financial distress could be more demoralizing than war (just consider that financial problems and the accompanying humiliations can lead to suicide, but war doesn't appear to do so directly)."

Taleb understated it. Not only does war not lead to suicide, it reduces it. (Money increases it, war reduces it.) Why?

Maybe it has something to do with transitioning into having a purpose. And something to do with how it feels to be a warrior.

Chapter 45

Produce something new and beautiful

I start each day with exercise and reading from inspirational written pieces I've saved over the years in case I forget, momentarily, how great and lively life was meant to be. They call it "life" for a reason.

They don't call life "trying to get by without too much anger or depression." That's not what you see when you hold a newly born baby. You see life.

We were born to be happy and great at what we do. Then we add stories and negative beliefs to that and things get sidetracked. But the time warrior will put things back on track instantly. With his morning reading. Back to *my* morning reading. This is the one that came up for me today:

Not a single person is born in the world who has not a certain capacity which will make him proud, who is not pregnant with something to produce, to give birth to something new and beautiful, to make the existence richer. There is not a single person who has come into the world empty.

Osho

Chapter 46

Your problem is not time management

When you say "I'm having a real problem with time management," my first objective is not to come up with some kind of better tips or techniques for you because that's really not what's at play.

What I want to find out is what's *beneath* the time management problem.

Because if you had a clear objective—let's say your objective was to go to the airport and fly to New York City—you would have no problem managing time.

You're on your way out the door to the car to drive to the airport and somebody says to you, "Hey, do you have a minute? I've got a couple of things I want to discuss." You simply say, "No, I don't. I don't have time right now, I'm on my way to the airport."

You are a warrior in that moment of time. You can say no.

Purpose makes you that way.

And you would get into your car and you would go to the airport, and maybe make an appointment to talk with that person later.

You wouldn't have any problem whatsoever managing your time! The reason for that is you have a specific mission. You have a commitment. People who have that don't have problems with time management because they always know what to say yes to and what to say no to.

I am always committed to getting to the airport on time to catch my plane. If a call comes in for me and somebody says "Maurice is on the line," I say "Tell him I'll call him from New York." And if somebody else says "Do you have a minute? I'd love to talk to you," I say "I don't, I'm sorry, I'm on my way to the airport."

So with a clear mission driving me, time management is never a problem. Even if my car breaks down, I grab a cab real fast so I can still get to the airport. Nothing gets in the way of me going to New York.

Now what if I could live each day that way!

I truly would not have any time management problems ever because I would be so on purpose and so focused that I'd always know when to say "no" and when to say "yes."

The problem comes when someone gets up in the morning, gets out of bed, and sleepily walks into the never-ending "demands" of their day with no sense of purpose or mission. There's no New York that day.

These people have nothing that they're up to and no primary goal. So when someone pokes their head in the office and says, "You got a minute?" the answer is always yes. Why would they say no? That wouldn't be very pleasing.

So I say yes to that, like I say yes to everyone, I open every email, I take every call. Pretty soon I'm falling behind with what I know I have to do and I then believe at the end of the day that I have a time management problem when I don't. I have a mission problem.

Soon I'll go around telling people "I have more to do than I have time to do it in!" Even though that's not really true. The truth is I have no direction.

With the people that I work with who have "time management problems," the first thing we create to counter it is boldness.

What's always missing is boldness—an ability to be brave and strong in staying on mission. We are on our way to New York.

Chapter 47

What gets measured gets done

People often ask how I write so many books. I didn't start until I was 49, and yet there are now 30 of them.

It's really a matter of choosing to do it or not to do it.

If I only work when I'm "inspired" my work won't be reliable, and it won't be accountable. It won't be a grown-up activity. I'll be like some kid always trying to decide something.

My problem with productivity only happens when I don't have a discipline. Because then I wake up every day *trying to decide* if I *feel like* doing it. And that's like waking up and trying to decide whether I "feel like" flying to New York, even though I have a ticket and a seat on the plane.

This New York state of mind can be done with anything that's important enough to you to remove from the world of feeling and place into the world of robotic accountability.

I was once hired to work with a team of sales people whose results were mediocre. When I walked into their sales offices for the first time I looked around and saw nothing on the walls. They had a white board on one wall but it only noted vacation times!

I turned to the sales manager and said, "One thing I'm sure of," and he looked at me questioningly as I said, "Vacations will be taken and they'll be taken on these certain days."

He asked me what I meant and I said that the most important thing that was missing from his workplace was a SCOREBOARD! Who's selling what? Who's leading the team? Who's in second place? Who had the best week? The best month?

Once we put up scoreboards, sales improved.

This was a move I learned from my own coach and mentor, Steve Hardison, who once went into an anemic company and boosted morale and sales almost overnight by filling an entire conference room's walls with massive scoreboards. They measured all sales activity and results daily!

What gets measured gets done.

Chapter 48

What about the fear factor?

I always used to think that *prior to* taking the action I wanted to take, I would have to do all kinds of personal growth work and change my level of courage.

Wow, not true!

It isn't courage I'm lacking prior to doing a big project. It's simply a system. And every good system includes some accountability.

So if I'm going to be in a weight-lifting contest, I want to have a person there in my training sessions who makes certain I lift the weights and holds the chart and watches me. That simply works for me. It works for all athletes. Kobe Bryant in his last playoff hired a coach (an extra coach) to coach him when practice was over to do certain things he never did before and that he couldn't trust himself to do on his own.

(Even though everyone says he already had an amazing work ethic.)

So the *result* was more important than *what it looked like*. A lot of people wonder what it would look like to get help. What would people think of me? That becomes a bigger concern than the result itself!

Does it look like I can't discipline myself? Does it look like I'm afraid to do it by myself?

If you want a result, you'll come up with a way to get the result. You won't care what *anything* looks like.

So what's really happening when I'm not getting a result is my not really wanting the result. What's really going on with me if I'm not making enough marketing calls (let's say) is that *I don't really want to make marketing calls.* That's it. End of story.

It's not as if I've got a fear of making marketing calls. That's not it! There are a lot of things that I want to do that I have fear around, but I do them anyway. It's just that I don't want the result.

What I always want to know is whether I really want something. Do I really want this? If I do, what would guarantee it? That's the real creative question.

If I want to paint five canvases between now and the end of the month, what would guarantee that this gets done? I would do something that would *guarantee* that. I might promise a gallery five canvases, I might take an advance payment for them so there's no way out, I might hire a guy to come in and chart my progress every day. Who knows, but I would somehow guarantee that I would do it.

I have a coach that I use, and I have used various coaches throughout my life. Whenever something occurred that that wasn't OK with me, I knew it really wasn't something wrong with my personality or what my parents didn't teach me. If I went down that road I'd stay stuck in it for a year. What was always missing was a guarantee.

One time I wasn't making enough sales calls and I went to a good friend of mine who is a hypnotherapist and I said I want you to hold me accountable. Every night I'm going to email you with how many sales calls I've made and I want you and me to talk once a month. You're going to talk to me about my performance. I'd built another level of accountability in for myself. I made it impossible for me to get out of it. *I wanted the results* more than I wanted to understand my defects.

Find someone in your world who would be willing to be a performance coach for you, someone to work with you to find out what it is that you want to do, and who will agree to hold you accountable for doing it.

Chapter 49

What are the steps I should take to overcome procrastination?

Do the things you're procrastinating on. Those are the steps I would take.

List three things you've procrastinated on. Do those three things. Those three things will be your first *three steps*. If you really want real steps that will always work in a guaranteed way.

Why didn't you do these things before now? Why do you care? I don't care if it was fear, laziness, or because your father never showed you how to do it. I don't care if it's a DNA imbalance on the right side of your spiral nebula.

I don't care about anything like that.

If procrastination is occurring, *do* the things you are procrastinating on. It's a very simple cure and it's the last thing people really want to do because they don't really want to cure procrastination. They want to find some mysterious psychotic fault line in themselves that *causes* them to procrastinate and then try to examine that fault line (even if it takes years) rather than do the thing.

Emerson has written many wonderful essays on this and one of the things he said is "Do the thing and you shall have the power." That's the opposite of what most people think. They think, "I don't seem to have the power to do the thing! That's my problem. I don't really have the willpower or the energy to DO THE THING!"

Well, OK, if you're a procrastinator on mowing the lawn or shoveling the walk, go do it. Then do it again, and do it again, and I promise you the procrastination will go away.

In his very poetic autobiography, *Speak, Memory,* Vladimir Nabokov wrote about his experience of life. He realized that true spiritual enlightenment came not in a passive dreamy state, but rather during the most intense action. People believe somehow that passivity and repose are the sources of vision. But Nabokov said no, "It is certainly not then—not in dreams—but when one is wide awake, at moments of robust joy and achievement, on the highest terrace of consciousness, that mortality has a chance to peer beyond its own limits."

Chapter 50

How does a warrior deal with job loss?

People often take forever to get a new job. They let emotions, imaginary "devastation" and all the attendant traditional hysteria they associate with job loss ruin their time efficiency in getting a new job.

If I want a job, or a contract, or a promotion, I want to do it with velocity, so that I'm not wallowing in limbo. I want to be more of a time warrior, not less. And just because I'm not employed or "on the clock" anywhere, it doesn't mean I have to suspend the warrior's approach.

The fastest way to get a new position is through the principle of the unexpected. I want to always do the unexpected—not the expected.

People do a job interview and then they try to anticipate what's expected. Do my potential employers expect a thank you note? A follow-up call? How many hours do I have before I have to thank them? Then they try to do what's expected. And there's no enthusiasm, or creativity, or joy in that.

So consider the person who is trying to decide whom to hire. If everybody they interview does what's expected, how do they know whom to hire? How do they know you're a special person? How do they know you are any different than all the other people who are applying?

If you really want a job that you're applying for, do extraordinary things. Send three thank-you notes, not one. Think of wild things to do. Think of things they don't expect, because the hardest thing for the person doing the hiring to find out is how much enthusiasm you really have for doing this job. They have no way of knowing unless you show them.

Show them, very dramatically, that you have more enthusiasm for doing the job than the other candidates. Show them you have more energy, more inventiveness, and you're not afraid to lose face in the name of getting that job.

Anyone doing less than that is not really, truly wanting that job.

Find a job you really want and apply for that one and then go crazy with your application. I've done wild things when I wanted a job—I've gotten jobs I was absolutely not qualified for in any way and I was told that it would be impossible for them to hire me. I would then do such extraordinary things to show them that it would be a mistake if they didn't hire me, that they hired me. I wasn't "qualified," so I qualified myself. That's the warrior's way. Anything else has me assume a victim identity at the worst possible time in my life to do so.

Chapter 51

There are no boring things in life

How would a time warrior handle the boring things that fill up a day? Like writing checks, doing laundry, putting things away, taking care of a pet and all that?

Well, a warrior does all small things with great effectiveness. She does it with inventiveness, humor and love.

She sings when she does the dishes, and she takes her sweet time when she lovingly writes checks (she really understands how nice it is to have the money to be sending people). She slows down and enjoys everything instead of having a category called boring.

If I continuously activate that "boring" category in my head it is going to be a long day. The day will be filled up with difficult work and I will feel dreary and distressed. I'll drag myself around wondering how I can get it all done.

What's boring is all up to me. It's completely in my control. I can do any task any way I want and I can have as much fun with it as I choose.

Chapter 52

The self-employed warrior

When we're newly out on our own, freshly self-employed, only answering to ourselves, it's usually a shock to the system.

Because when we worked for other people, we let them rule the day. We'd show up and go where they wanted us to go. They would manage us, and then we would reluctantly do good work inside that structure.

But now that we are off on our own, the challenge is different. Because we don't know what to do. And creative people need some kind of structure. That is, if they are going to have productive days.

When I write a book without a writing schedule, it is really a nightmare, and it doesn't get done right, and I end up at the end of the deadline working overtime. In the end, it's not good work, and it's not creative writing.

Paradoxically, the best creativity comes from working with the most structure you can possibly impose on yourself.

Anything you can do to schedule yourself increases creative output. You think it would take away your spontaneity, but it really doesn't. It's amazing how well an artificial structure works. Forcing the action. It works in all aspects of life. I don't feel like going to this meeting... I don't feel like going to this family gathering... I dread it. And then I get there and I have the time of my life.

So now I just do it. Because it's on this structure I call a calendar.

What do I feel like doing right now? That is the worst question I could ever ask myself during my workday.

On a weekend that's a fine question. "What do I feel like doing? I'll watch a little baseball, I'll play the guitar." That's fine, but in my workday, the feeling question is the worst question I can ask myself. The best questions are: "What do I want to produce?" and "What structure would guarantee that?"

Chapter 53

How to love putting things off

Keep in mind that some people like doing things at the last minute.

When I have clients who wait until the last minute to do things, they usually criticize themselves for it. But why? Some people just like doing it that way! You don't have to demonize that. You don't have to give that a negative label if you don't want to.

I like to work to last minute deadlines myself. I enjoy that. It's fun for me. I love the challenge. I love the game of it.

I remember when I worked for a newspaper (remember what those were?). There'd be a deadline and we'd be going to press at a certain time and there'd be a breaking story and they would need my article by 11 o'clock that night in order to get it into the next edition. I would love that. The adrenaline was great. It was the same when I studied in college—when my question was, "Why would I read that book now when the test is over a week away?"

I would love studying that way. I don't have to make that wrong if I don't want to. I can say, "Yeah, I love that. It's the way I play life. I like pressured deadlines."

With a recent book I wrote, the publisher said, "Whenever it's finished, just tell us. We don't have a publishing deadline for this. You take your time. You just let us know when it's finished."

So I didn't have an external deadline, but I don't enjoy that. So I said, "Here's when I promise you I will have the finished manuscript," and then I gave them a date. I set up deadlines all along the way and I hit every one of them at the last minute and I loved doing it. People are so quick (and I think it comes out of childhood) to find negative interpretations for everything they do. I'm a procrastinator... I'm not organized... But then by thinking that, they lose energy. Their mood gets negative and now they feel even less like doing things and it's just a downward slope.

Why not say, "Hey, I love deadlines, I love the adrenaline...It's how I work. What do you have for me?"

Nobody criticizes a quarterback for winning a game in overtime. They don't say, "He procrastinated! He should have won it in regulation time!"

Chapter 54

You can be the author of urgent

People often tell me they are upset with themselves because they only do what's urgent and never get around to doing what's important.

But they forget one thing. They get to make things urgent whenever they want.

The problem arises in thinking that I, myself, don't get to declare anything urgent. I don't have the right. I'm not the ultimate judge of what's urgent. Other people are. Other people's demands.

If somebody needs a document by a certain time it qualifies as an "urgent" task because it's coming from somebody else. If I, myself, have an important task to do, because it's about me and it's only important to me, it cannot be urgent.

Can you see the weakness in that system?

When I live that way I've got priorities backwards.

Let's say I was going to write a poem for my friend for her birthday, and that's important to me, so I want to mark it urgent. I'll now say that's going to get done today. I'm not even going to answer my phone or look at my screen until that poem gets written because I've decided it's my priority.

Is it urgent in anyone else's mind? Who cares? They don't count right now—if I'm living authentically. Others don't count compared to this job right now because I'm the author of my life story. I'm the author of this novel called my life and I'm not going to give that up. I'm not going to pretend I'm not the author. (The word "authentic" and the word "author" come from the same place.)

I get to say when anything's urgent and when it's not. "URGENT" doesn't always have to be some external thing that somebody's going to get mad at me about if it's not done.

That's the little kid in me living my life instead of the adult in me. That's the infantile part of me that's scared of other people. Most people use a child's viewpoint to create their daily priorities: would someone else get mad if I didn't do it by this time?

But the warrior captures the concept of urgent and makes it useful instead of stressful.

Chapter 55

Recovering from overwhelm

Your problem is not that you are overwhelmed. Your problem is an attachment to the story of overwhelm.

Truthfully, are you overwhelmed? Or do you just feel that way? Let us really, really look at your last five days. Let's just isolate one of the hours. Let's take a look at this "overwhelm" and see if it's really there.

You are not, in this hour we've chosen to look at, at all overwhelmed, are you? Not in this particular hour. But your story is that you are.

You can drop that story. You can tell a different story. Try this story: "I've only got one thing to do! How liberating. It's the thing I'm doing right now."

Chapter 56

Willpower, or the choosing to begin it?

Begin—to begin is half the work, let half still remain;
again begin this, and thou wilt have finished.

Marcus Aurelius

I've never seen anyone without any willpower. People have all the willpower they would ever want or need. It's sitting there inside of them ready to be called upon at all times. Even children have almost limitless willpower.

So what's actually missing is a choice. The choice to do it.

Let's say I have a bunch of drudgery and legal work that I've promised myself I'll do by tomorrow and I notice I'm not doing it.

That's not because of lack of willpower.

That's only because I have not chosen to start it yet.

I haven't started the game called doing it! So I haven't set up the circumstance and talked to myself so that it would get started. The minute I tell myself, "I'm doing this," (followed by simultaneous *action* of some sort, any sort) I've got all the willpower I would ever need.

Willpower was never missing.

What was missing was my *move* to get it started. A simple choice to jump in and start this. That was missing.

Willpower is merely the force you can call on anytime you need to get something done—once you've chosen to start doing it. So when I decide to start walking to the store, nothing else matters. I can be tired, but that won't matter. Maybe I haven't slept in two nights, but that won't matter. The circumstance can be anything in the world, but the minute I choose to walk to the store, I walk to the store, because I automatically utilize my willpower to do it. I've got a limitless amount of willpower following any clear choice.

The real issue in life is the choices I am making.

So what's this desire I have to want it to be about willpower? Why do I want my lack of action to be about a "thing" inside me I don't have? The answer is this: I would rather find and identify some defect in myself than take that first step. Isn't that the easier, softer way to live? Identifying flaws and defects all day?

Many people have adopted a very popular story: "I'm a procrastinator who doesn't have much willpower." Well, the game's over then. You're out of luck. You'll never get what you want in life. You'll never succeed. Because you believe you don't have the basic qualities you need to do it.

That's the easiest way out, but it's all a mind game. Why do you want out of this game? Why not win this game?

Whatever it is you are not doing, notice that you are *choosing* not to do it. There's no defect in you! There's the opposite of a defect. There is, instead, a power. A power to choose. Choose to, choose not to, same power. Always power. There's nothing wrong with you. There's no weakness. There's no lack of willpower. There's no gene for procrastination. It's always a conscious choice.

Let's say I decide to walk to the store and it's two miles away. Once I choose to walk to the store I put my shoes on and head out the door. Getting to the store? No problem. Starting toward the store? The only problem there could ever be.

Chapter 57

What if I don't know what I'm supposed to do?

A client named Priscilla came to me and said, "What am I supposed to do to manage my time?"

I said, "Why do you want to manage your time?"

Priscilla was stumped. And then she said, "Isn't time management important? Always? I just don't know what I'm *supposed* to do."

I wanted her to find her purpose first. With a powerful enough purpose, time gets managed by itself. Like the trip to New York we talked about.

And once she finds her purpose, we might address the other part of her question: What am I *supposed to* do?

I would want her to stop asking that question. I'd want her to always be careful about wanting her life to contain things she is "supposed to" do. That is a major warning sign that she is about to have a very unfulfilling life.

Having your mind think it's "supposed to" do certain things takes you all the way back to dependent childhood. It rockets you into an infantile world of no power.

Now you're in the world of *supposed to*. Planet Supposed To! On that planet you are the child and the rest of the world is grown up. It's where you waste all your time trying to learn what you're *supposed to be doing.*

The premise of that *supposed to* question is that you don't have any of your own creativity or power—so you can't choose anything for yourself.

Let's always turn that around.

Instead of "What am I supposed to do?" how about asking yourself, "What do I **want** to do?"

Chapter 58

What if things break down?

There will be days that have the potential to confuse you.

(Actually it's only your thinking that can confuse you, but let's say there will be days. Let's acknowledge that even your Mama said there'd be days.)

You'll have your day all planned out and then your computer crashes. Now you're spending hours trouble-shooting, which puts you behind on everything else.

Then the car doesn't start and again, you're dealing with that and it's keeping you away from what needs to be done, so you feel like you're spinning your wheels and getting behind. So how do you deal with feeling behind?

You don't have to feel behind.

The other day I had a meeting planned with a client. It was an important meeting. But I was hit by a bad stomach flu. I really couldn't leave home. So I called the client and re-scheduled.

Now I'm behind, right? Because now I have to re-schedule. Now I'm not able to complete that meeting in a timely fashion, so of course I'm behind!

But do I have to feel behind? Not if I remember that "behind" is just an optional concept. If I buy the concept then "behind" becomes a feeling. It's a feeling caused by a thought that says I should be further ahead than this. But that's just a passing thought I've chosen to believe. I don't have to believe it.

What if I were okay with the fact that life happens? Computers crash, stomachs get upset, cars break down, flights are delayed, a kid gets sick and I have to pick her up at school. Life happens, and I love it. I can dance with anything.

I'm never behind. I'm never ahead. I'm just happy here and now in a non-linear way.

"Behind" and "ahead" both require a linear life. A view of life as a long measuring tape. A tapeworm! There's no opportunity in that kind of life. There's just dreary trudging along the path, sometimes ahead, usually behind. Who wants to live that way?

My choice is always to either (1) Live that way on a horizontal tapeworm line, facing one damn thing after another or (2) RISE UP into the vertical world of pure creative opportunity sometimes known as "now."

Chapter 59

Creative means you have Plan B

Plan B is a very creative thing. Very adult, very mature, and a wise thing to always have in place. I always have a Plan B.

(And, by the way, when I say I "always" do something, like I am the example everyone should follow, please keep in mind that most of this has taken me many, many years—most of you are a lot younger than I am, and you are way ahead of me. I'm not lording over you saying I'm the one you should be like—it took me years to learn to do this! And you can do this stuff right now. And you won't have to tell people it took you years. You can say you picked it up in a heartbeat.)

If something breaks down and I can't do what I was going to do with my time, I love to have a Plan B. Even in small matters. I always take an extra book to read with me everywhere I go in case things don't go like they're supposed to. I always take extra audio programs in my car so that if traffic gets slow, I'm not upset—it becomes a great opportunity to listen and learn. Or listen and sing.

You can use Plan B for bigger things than that. Like your primary employment. When I have coaching clients who are worried about their employer I ask, "What's your other job? Your next job? Your plan B?"

"I didn't think I needed one," they say.

You don't "need" one, but life is great when you have one. When you have a Plan B that you are creating on the side, then everything in life becomes, "This or something better."

Chapter 60

The future consumes time and energy

*Never let anyone come to you without coming away
better and happier.*

Mother Teresa

She said that work without love is slavery. She said,
repeatedly, that it is not what we *do*, but how much love
we put into doing it. She said preoccupation with the
future is always a mistake.

She said future worries "take the love out of
everything."

I love reading about the long and eventful life of
Mother Teresa, a woman who kept insisting that joy in
this present moment *is* strength. And worrying about the
future is the very definition of weakness.

And, as business efficiency expert Kerry Gleeson has
noted, "The constant, unproductive preoccupation with
all the things we have to do in the future, is the single
largest consumer of time and energy."

Slow down. Focus. And love what you are doing.

Chapter 61

Learning to welcome everything

Imagine a life in which you are welcoming every circumstance.

There are times in people's lives when they *perceive* life in such a way—when they are in a good enough mood, when things are "breaking their way,"—that whatever circumstance appears, whether on the news or over the phone, they welcome it.

In those wonderful moments they realize that it's always a matter of perception.

Lindsay Brady's profound book on hypnosis, *As the Pendulum Swings*, presents the best explanation of perception I've yet read. Brady has discovered, after working with over 20,000 clients, that perception is what drives human behavior. We behave based on how we perceive things—not based on how things really "are."

Let's say you are afraid of snakes. You think snakes are creepy and you have a funny feeling that they are dangerous to you. You don't want one in your home. But you are sitting in your home and you notice a snake has entered your home!

Now look at how you behave. Look at your actions. Look at your thoughts. There is panic, there is a scramble. Soon you are fleeing your own home! You might be crawling out the window, then calling 911, or calling animal control, yelling, heart pounding. Your wild behavior is something we could put on YouTube and call it One Definite Way of Behaving When a Snake Enters Your Home. And your way may even be the most common way.

But now imagine that you are a biologist.

You have specialized in snakes and they are the animals you most enjoy working with. Your true love. You've studied them, you've worked with them in the laboratory, you've been with them on farms and now you are sitting at home and you notice that one has entered your home.

Because you know about snakes, you can see that this snake is perfectly harmless. You have identified it right away. So that when you see it, you actually light up. You think, "Oh, my goodness, take a look at that, what a beautiful specimen!"

Because you know about snakes you might get some kind of food (you know what they love), you might lure it over to a little cage you keep for just this kind of occasion.

Now the snake comes toward you and you put a little food out there and the snake comes toward it and you gather the snake up in your hands and you hold it lovingly and you admire it and you say, "Boy, what a beautiful specimen—what a sweet little boy this is."

You hold it for a while, feel its warmth, feel its nice smooth skin, admiring it. Now you place it in the cage. You clasp the door. You're going to rescue it back outside where it belongs after looking at it for a while and enjoying the entire experience. You might even call a biologist colleague and say, "You'll never guess who just came into my house."

Look at those two different ways of responding to the snake. So different. The *circumstance* here was the same: *snake enters house*. But the perception was different, and you can see that the perception was what drove the two opposite kinds of behavior.

In our lives we have all kinds of "circumstances" like job loss, marital argument, death in the family, health difficulties, divorce, wild weather... all kinds of circumstances occur.

Are they good circumstances? Are they bad? It depends on our perception. How we act and feel are not caused by the circumstances but rather by our perception of them.

The perception you have of anything is always what drives your feelings and your actions and your thoughts.

So, would you be more effective managing circumstance or managing perception? Which would change your life faster and more effectively?

This is why linear time management usually fails us. It doesn't recognize the power of perception. It keeps trying to rearrange circumstance.

Let's look at another example. The football stadium is packed with people. Let's say it's Michigan versus Michigan State. So half the stadium is cheering for Michigan State—Go Spartans! The other half of the stadium is cheering for Michigan—Go Wolverines! At the end of the game, after Michigan wins, the Michigan half of the stadium is cheering and hugging and celebrating and laughing and clapping each other on the back!

But the other half of the stadium looks downhearted. Maybe they say, "Wait till next year," but they're in a bad mood.

Did you notice that the circumstance was identical? The same game was played on that field for both sides. Yet half of the people (because of their perception that "it's good when our team wins") are happy and jumping around while the other half mopes.

Behavior always flows from perception. And the good news here is that I can change perception. Circumstance can be anything. I can keep shifting my perception of that circumstance until it's in alignment with my mission.

I have people tell me, "I'm down because I'm going through a divorce right now." Or, "I'm down because of the global economy." Or, "I'm down because my daughter is involved with the wrong people." Or, "I'm down because my business has gone in a bad direction."

They have made a logical mistake. They have misread how the brain works when they attribute their feelings to outer-world causes. It would be more accurate to say, "I'm down because I'm forming a perception that this is bad."

We bring ourselves down when we perceive a circumstance as bad and we bring ourselves up when we perceive a circumstance as good.

If we could see that it's within our power to switch perceptions then we'd be free to create the day we want.

A warrior doesn't hang on to disempowering perceptions. So why do I?

It really is the definition of insanity to fool myself into feeling this bad. Because by feeling bad, I'm now not performing very well. I'm not being effective, and I'm not solving problems or creating solutions. I'm just discouraged. Now I'm short with people—not returning their calls and creating a real mess around myself.

Soon I'll call this mess a time management problem!

Non-linear time management allows me to create my best energy for everything. I can choose to perceive *every* circumstance as an opportunity to grow and stay on my mission. And if this opportunity is also challenging, that's even better. I have a chance to rise up—like a kite rises against the wind.

If there's no wind the kite can't fly. Have you ever tried to fly a kite when there's no wind at all? Have you ever tried to have a great life when there's no challenge? If there's no challenge for me I cannot become stronger. I cannot grow.

When I learn about perception I learn about myself. I find out how to become more resourceful. I do fewer frivolous things. I'm not blind any more. I'm not spending money without thinking. I'm not unconscious to opportunity any more.

We have a whole nation right now that forgot to learn about cause-and-effect economics. We were so giddy with false abundance (easy credit) for so long, we simply forgot the dynamic of reality. We perceived that economic principles were for other people. "That's for politicians! They'll take care of us!" Learning them and living them was too much of a challenge.

And look at what came crashing down.

But whenever something comes crashing down something else can start building up. And that's where I want my mind to go: What's good about this? What's great about this? What strengthens me? What can make me better?

Here's a fresh option of perception: These are good times *because* they are challenging, not *in spite of the fact* that they are challenging. These times are my wake-up call. This is where I get my true strength. This is where I find out what I am made of. Who would not want to find out what they're made of?

Chapter 62

Work itself is what inspires us

Just as appetite comes by eating,
so work brings inspiration,
if inspiration is not discernible at the beginning.

Igor Stravinsky

The great composer and conductor Stravinsky was in on a great secret. Inspiration will arrive *after* you start working on the thing you thought you weren't inspired by.

Most people think they are not inspired because their project is not inherently inspiring. Therefore they procrastinate. Or they just work on it sporadically. They don't realize that if they would slow down and do this project one slow step at a time—in a loving and deeply energetic way—inspiration might just appear. After the work starts!

Because there's inspiration everywhere.

It's sleeping in everything. You don't have to worry about it any more. Just get to work and watch what happens.

"As a cure for worrying, work is better than whiskey," said Emerson.

Now you tell me!

Because I tried whiskey as a cure for worrying. For years. And you can't say I didn't give it a fair trial. Years, I gave it. Did it cure worry? It made it worse. Turned worry into deep fears.

Then, after getting clean and sober through my program and the grace of God, I tried other cures for worry. Other ways of going unconscious and disconnecting myself from reality. Never realizing how wonderful reality was!

Then I tried—when there was nothing else left to try—Emerson's way. Wow. Worries leave when I get into action.

Chapter 63

Are you fearless or brave?

There's a huge difference between being fearless and being brave. Being brave is often quite admirable, especially when you are standing up for a principle despite what everyone thinks.

But being brave means you are still overriding and overcoming a fear, so there's battle inside. Being fearless is very different. Being fearless means there is no battle. Just relaxed focus.

This is the very reason why the samurai taught their warriors to "die before going into battle"—so that they wouldn't have to be brave in battle, but could be playful, freewheeling and fearless. They were less likely to die that way.

Most people have confusion about the word "fearless." They think fearless means "brave" or "courageous," but it's nothing like that.

In fact, it's not even similar to that. Being fearless is absolute peace. It suggests an easy connection to the universe. And there's no worry. There's no feeling of fear whatsoever.

There are so many things we do throughout the day in an unknowingly fearless way that we don't appreciate the reality of fearlessness. When we are loving a person, or enjoying an activity—playing a song on the piano, reading something we enjoy, or jogging, or playing volleyball—we often experience fearlessness.

I remember when I first started giving speeches years ago. I had a huge fear of public speaking. I was terrified of being up in front of an audience. It was a lifelong fear! I would get in front of an audience and it would feel like an elephant was standing on my chest and something was constricting my throat. My knees were weak. I couldn't get my breath. Total fear—and I pushed on and I was brave anyway and I walked out and there were a hundred people waiting for me to talk. My voice was shaky, my hands were sweating—and I spoke anyway. Now that's courage. That's being brave. That's being bold and that's forging ahead in the face of fear. (A rare event in my life!)

But it was completely different from being fearless.

I talked to a group the other night where there were 900 people in the audience. I remember walking up on the stage and feeling nothing but peaceful energy and love. I wasn't afraid. Those days were gone! That fear left me years ago.

So there *is* a possibility of being fearless about anything and everything. If there were no possibility, I would not have written a book called *Fearless.* I would not get people's hopes up. I would not get my own hopes up.

Chapter 64

Let your life be a small thing

Great things are not done by impulse, but by a series of
small things brought together.

Vincent van Gogh

I love the way life coach Rich Litvin talks about confidence. Especially the part where he says he asks his clients to dream a really big dream and once they do that, to take the tiniest action possible, the smallest step imaginable in the pursuit of that dream.

As he explains so well, it's not a choice between success and failure in living the dream, it's a choice, today, between a tiny step and no step.

Chapter 65

How functional is inspiration?

How do I get someone else in my life to experience the changes that I've experienced?

What would have this change occur?

Well, I know I can't control another person. So my only shot is through being a model and example—motivation through inspiration.

If I am leading a team of people and I want them to change their behavior then I want to *be* who I want them to be. I want to show them what that's like. If they see me with a customer or a sales prospect, I want to demonstrate what it's like to love the customer, to sell to the prospect in the same way I want them to do it. I want to inspire them. I don't want to teach them, fix them or correct them.

People love being inspired. They watch the Olympics and get inspired. They see people sing on YouTube and get inspired. They watch the movie *Secretariat* and get inspired. People can be inspired by a horse!

If you see the movie *Secretariat* you may wonder why you cried throughout when there was nothing sad in the movie. What was all the crying about? I was crying, people around me were crying. About this horse called Big Red. Later named Secretariat.

Was the horse shot or put down?

No! He retired peacefully to romp in the field with the ladies.

Then why is it such a moving movie that has all of us crying?

I may have written the answer to this in an earlier book, and I may not have. But please see the movie to find the answer. And take anyone with you who needs a good cry, but not a sad cry. It might be a cry of raging joy, the tears that come when the soul sees itself for the first time. Tears of inspiration.

We weep for the part of us that does not give its all.

During the Olympics, people enroll in health clubs at a much higher rate than before. How beautiful it is to express yourself through your body and exercise. How thrilling to experience energy at such a level.

My own enrollment in the health club didn't happen from somebody criticizing me for being overweight and sitting on the couch. It happened from watching the Olympics and becoming inspired.

So the route to helping anybody—a pessimist, a victim, anybody—is by working on myself and having my life be more inspiring for people.

That's what lets people have a chance at change. They want to *see* it. They don't want to hear what's wrong with them. They want to see what's right in you. They don't want to hear why they're weak or why they're inadequate. They want to watch and see a more exciting way and be inspired and have it be *their* idea to change—not yours.

That's why the famous quote from Gandhi endures. "Don't change other people. Be the change you wish to see in other people."

Chapter 66

A warrior brings the light

Here's something that helped me understand the created nature of the time warrior. She dies, like a samurai, before going into battle.

To understand that better, let's look again at the concept of darkness. Darkness isn't anything. Darkness is merely the absence of light, and when I bring light into the room there is no more darkness.

I didn't have to *overcome* the darkness. I didn't have to *remove* the darkness. Darkness is nothing at all. It's the absence of light.

Well, fear is the same thing. Fear is the absence of love. If I fear public speaking it's because I don't yet love public speaking.

I don't have to *overcome* the fear, battle the fear, be brave, and feel the fear and do it anyway. If enough love comes in, there is no more fear. Fear wasn't anything to begin with but the absence of love.

Fear and love are opposites in many ways just like darkness and light are opposites as concepts. So what occurs when fear disappears is the same thing as when darkness disappears.

I light a candle, I turn on the light, there is no more darkness.

So how did I turn on the light as far as talking in front of groups? Well, I practiced. I did it again and again. I built up the *love* of it, and with enough love there's no more fear. (With enough practice, there is more than enough love.) Anything you do over and over in a lovingly, repetitive way makes fear disappear like darkness disappears.

There are other ways to make fear disappear as well.

Enlightenment, for example. Someone becomes en*light*ened and now there's nothing to fear.

I finally understood, when I was little, that there was no monster under my bed—I was no longer afraid. I really got it. The light had come on.

Byron Katie uses an example that Ramana Maharshi used. You walk along in the desert and you think there is a rattlesnake in front of you and you feel huge fear. You get closer and now you see it's not a rattlesnake—it's a rope. Seeing that it's a rope, you are enlightened to it being a rope. So there's nothing to be afraid of. You can look at that rope a hundred times and it just can't scare you.

That's the enlightenment route to having fear disappear—it's a form of bringing the light.

I can have enlightenment or I can have loving practice. Each one works. Fear disappears. I'm feeling fearless. In other words, there are no feelings there at all other than timeless love and joy.

Chapter 67

Time is money and money is time

Sometimes my trouble with time is really my trouble with money.

If you have a real fear about money, the first things to look at are the underlying beliefs you carry. You might say, "I could lose my job. And I couldn't handle it if that happened."

So let's look at what would happen if you lost your job. How bad would that be? Is it really true that *you couldn't handle it* if it happened?

Might you not survive if it happened? I mean, maybe you *could* handle it. It might be uncomfortable, but I think you could handle it.

People get very confused when they tell themselves they couldn't handle something. They scare themselves unnecessarily by believing that thought.

It's like believing in your future devastation. You think, "I would be devastated!" But would you? Maybe the worst thing you would go through would be discomfort. A little bit of confusion, anxiety, and discomfort. That's it.

But you don't realize that. Because of how you talk to yourself about the future. Because of the thoughts you believe about devastation and things you could not handle. You are unwilling to look back over your life and see that you have always been able to handle everything. Always. No exceptions.

Believing I couldn't handle various future scenarios reduces my energy for life. My effectiveness drops. Now I'm avoiding tasks I used to handle with ease. I even think I might have a time management problem because so many of these tasks pile up unfinished.

But I really just have a belief problem.

Most of these unnecessarily catastrophic beliefs are about money. I behave as if money were oxygen. I think losing all my money would be like having the oxygen taken out of the room. Now I won't be able to breathe any more! Terrifying picture. In the mind.

A warrior realizes money is not oxygen.

Money is a tool of value-exchange created through service. And service is something a warrior can always do.

Chapter 68

Creation versus attraction

Foster and polish the warrior spirit
while serving in the world;
illuminate the path
according to your inner light.

Morihei Ueshiba

Money is the perfect teacher of what I call the law of creation.

And it's important to see how the law of creation is different from the law of attraction.

The law of attraction is a very popular thing. There are many people who give seminars on it. *The Secret* is all about the law of attraction, and it's a wonderful law to know about. Because picturing things and creating your vision is a powerful, positive, first step in getting results.

The Book of Proverbs says, "Where there is no vision, the people will perish."

But the problem with the law of attraction is that it doesn't go all the way. It doesn't, all by itself, bring into existence what I want to bring into existence. It's just the first step. It just allows me to perceive it and picture it as an outcome I'd like to produce.

However! The law of *creation* is a law that's really fun to experience because it does go all the way. Follow it, and you get the result you are after.

The law of creation begins by re-focusing all power inside me. It has me as the initiator. I am the cause. I am the source of what results I want to produce in my life. Because of this, it's a warrior's law.

This law has me waking up and asking myself what would I like to *create*, not attract. What would I like to *produce* today? And from that question, I can design my day. I can plan the conversations I want to have with people who can move my goal forward with me. I can create my life. That's an exciting way to use my day.

The other way to live is the law of attraction, which is incomplete, or the law of *reaction,* which is even worse. The law of reaction has me thinking that other people have all the power and I need to somehow manipulate them to get them to approve of me.

If I spend my day doing nothing but pleasing others and trying to win their approval, I could end up without anything. I could end up resenting other people deeply because I've done all these things for them to no avail! In fact, they don't even trust me. They have seen through my manipulator's agenda. I've tried to please them but in the process I've turned them off.

Bad use of my time? Yes. Turning people off instead of turning them on? Badly misspent time. Worst use of time there is.

True, effective service that makes a difference in people's lives turns them on and gives you everything you could ever want. (Right there in the doing of it.)

Chapter 69

Childhood fears become adult beliefs

Most of our belief systems and therefore most of our fears originated in childhood. They are carry-overs. So it frees my life up when I look at those unquestioned, adopted underlying beliefs as the source of all my fear.

And when I say "adopted," I mean adopted. All those fearful beliefs are adopted from others. We overhear them. We also pick them up from movies and TV and popular novels. All the tragic, terrifying beliefs.

As we are learning what to fear, we also learn how to get protection. Protection comes from pleasing our parents, guardians, teachers, camp counselors and adult authorities with our "good" behavior. We win their approval by being "good." Our parents tell us, "You were *good* today!"

Maybe you, as a parent, say that to your child. And if the little child hears that it means she won your approval. She was pleasing to you. That's what that means. It doesn't mean she made a difference or served someone, or that she did something creative or heroic.

Heroic activities are rarely encouraged or honored in childhood. Children have to discover them later in life, and then only if they are ready for experimenting with a warrior's philosophy.

When a parent told you as a child, "You were so good today," that meant you didn't embarrass your parent.

As children we noticed right away that the grown-ups held the keys to everything we ever wanted. If we wanted to watch a movie, or wanted to have a friend spend the night, or wanted to have some orange juice, or wanted to buy something—it was up to the grown-ups. Always. Because grown-ups had all the power. Like kings and queens, they granted us things or they didn't. That's how it looked to us, anyway.

No wonder our primary practice and skill became how to please them! No wonder our first experience of mastery was in anticipating moods of others and learning to win their approval.

Some people move from that level of mastery to others. They leave pleasing behind and learn to serve in powerful ways. They become heroic and creative, too.

But they are the exception.

Most people stay stuck in a version of childhood forever. You even see them in nursing homes at the ends of their lives using little child voices to ask nurses for things. It never ends unless life itself ends.

Do you blame them? It was what they spent years and years training themselves to do! It's no longer even conscious. They just wake up and do it all day long. Even when it doesn't work.

If I've trained myself throughout my life to place my highest survival value on being non-threatening, accommodating, not making waves, not standing out, being like everyone else—then that becomes the belief system I take into adulthood. How could it not be? How could I not carry that over? How could I just drop that?

I can never drop that without challenging it. Which is where the whole warrior approach comes in. I now want to learn to challenge every belief.

Because with the old, fearful belief system, how could I fearlessly create my day? How could I even start to be a time warrior? How could I be anything but a passive, frightened child in a grown-up world?

But once I shift I can *be* the grown-up! My life now starts to work. That's why the term "warrior" is the only useful word for time management, because warrior is the most extreme grown-up position.

Children can't be warriors.

Chapter 70

There is no such thing as worthiness

People who don't feel worthy—people who tell me they spend a lot of time worrying about their "worthiness issues"—can experience a huge amount of freed up time once they realize that worthiness doesn't even exist.

How can you have an issue with something that doesn't exist?

Let's say I'm feeling unworthy and I wish I was worthy. How could I ever find out whether I was worthy? Who will give me the word? There isn't a worthiness center I can go to like a motor vehicle department where I can check on my worthiness, is there?

"How worthy am I?"

"Well, let me call it up on the screen. Just a minute please. What's your Social Security number? Thank you. It says here on a scale of 1 to 10, you are a 3. You're not very worthy. How do you justify asking people for money?"

Trying to feel worthy or "deserving" is sitting back and letting other people judge me. So I'm now sitting back in fear. "Do people think I deserve this?" Which is a child's thought. That's a little kid thinking that grown-ups have all the power.

Try taking a warrior's sword to all of that. Eliminate the dual time-wasters of worthiness and deserving. Two concepts that eat up precious time. That precious time could have been spent serving and prospering!

I'm actually someone who has struggled with this more than most people. My stories and my case history, covered in my previous books, exposed how bad this can get—and how bad life can get by operating out of this belief system that says the grown-ups have all the power and money.

It sounds in your mind like this: "I'm not a grown-up... I'm still a child... I don't deserve it... I need to know my worthiness before I charge anything... I need to please my parents before I save money."

All those thoughts and beliefs that make life so unnecessarily scary and painful.

But there is also a lot of great humor in all of this. Because, ultimately, it's not a tragic thing. A ruined life is full of funny stories. And if the warrior emerges from it, then all the stories of the past can now help other people in powerful ways. They can show other people that they can really be financially fearless. They don't have to struggle and worry and live life in such pain.

But if I don't take up the sword, how will it end? When's the pain going to end? In the nursing home? In the final hospital moments when there's a drip IV that tries to use pharmaceuticals to numb or suffocate the fear that's still pounding in me?

"Have I left enough money behind? Can I pay for this? Do I deserve to be loved?"

Let's get off that linear path of worthiness issues that stretches from birth to death. Let's rise up and live now. Do I deserve to rise up? Am I worthy? Those are just concepts, an idle person's mental playthings. They have nothing to do with a life of action.

Chapter 71

Stop forcing things to happen

The individual human mind is like a computer terminal connected to a giant database. The database is human consciousness itself, of which our own consciousness is merely an individual expression, but with its roots in the common consciousness of all mankind. This database is the realm of genius; because to be human is to participate in the database, everyone by virtue of his birth has access to genius.

David R. Hawkins
Power Versus Force

I love Hawkins' book because he makes such a great case for finding the inner power in you that was there all along. For using the genius you already have instead of trying to force the outside world to conform to your longings (wants and wishes)... Longings caused by deficits of inner peace.

True creative power always comes from within.

And power is so much more, well... *powerful* than force.

We have extreme time management problems when we are forcing things into our schedule and trying to do too much at once. Soon we're just playing around on the computer, visiting strange, alluring blog sites and off-mission entirely. This caving in to distraction comes from forcing.

The samurai uses a sword. The warrior carves out devoted time. Uninterrupted time that's reserved for a certain project or activity in a very devoted way. (The principle of devoted time is worth repeating as many times as necessary.) Time carved out and devoted. That's the best time to do anything important. That's when true, pure power emerges: inside devoted time.

Chapter 72

Looking for the perfect lover

We waste time looking for the perfect lover,
instead of creating the perfect love.

Tom Robbins

This observation of Mr. Robbins, who wrote *Even Cowgirls Get the Blues,* is precise and true in my experience.

We waste time looking for the perfect lover instead of creating. We waste time looking for happiness instead of making someone else happy. We waste time looking for purpose when it's right here in front of us. We fall in love with stories instead of people. We fall in love with a story called wealth instead of life's wealth.

And then, as if to wake us up, wealth and love stop coming in. So we switch lovers. We seek new employers. Always looking down the long linear road for a better future.

If you want this to end, it's time to go non-linear; to carve out a sacred *now* and stay inside it until you create the perfect love, the perfect life.

Chapter 73

Well-begun is half-done

The beginning is half of every action.

Greek proverb

The problem with procrastination is that there's no beginning going on. If there were a beginning happening there would be no procrastination.

Our problem isn't that we don't do something. It's that we don't begin it. Maybe because we are believing something negative about the task we are putting off, we don't begin. If we were not believing that belief we'd have already begun!

Poor time management, therefore, is always a problem of belief. What thought am I believing about this task that makes me unwilling to even start? Unless I am willing to challenge that thought quite thoroughly I will always suffer from this thing we call procrastination.

Remember that there are two ways a warrior can execute a successful challenge. One is internal, one is external. Internal: Write the belief down and thoroughly challenge its truth. External: Push the thought aside, push all thought aside, and just start the darn thing whether you feel like doing it or not.

When I work with clients who suffer from procrastination we work with the belief systems that create the problem. We challenge a thought like a philosopher challenges a precept: with a fearless confrontation of the "truth" of the negative belief.

Then we challenge like a warrior challenges. By simply *beginning* the task we were putting off, and finding out by doing so that well-begun is half-done.

Chapter 74

Passion to transform your world

Contained within the human heart is an inextinguishable drive to make greater sense of our world while also cultivating the freedom, passion and capacities to transform it.

Ken Wilber

Most linear time management systems cancel out the possibilities of freedom and passion.

They leave out everything the great contemporary philosopher Ken Wilber teaches about. Here he is talking further: "I'm sure you have noticed that while living integrally starts as something you know, it proceeds to something you do, and ends as something you embody. It is embodiment, this final step, that we all seek—the 'on-board capacities' to grow anywhere we want to; to live completely, deeply in touch with our unique gifts and vision. Not merely as something we know, but also as something we are."

This is it exactly. The primary question! Is our transformation something we *know* or is it something we *are*?

When I went into recovery from alcohol and addiction I found something in my life I'll just call spirit. I didn't find it in the long, linear future, but rather in a brand new understanding of this thing we all call "today."

"You mean I can never drink again?" I asked.

"Nothing says that," they said.

"But to be clean and sober must mean that. Never again! Not even on New Year's Eve? Not even if someone dies or I win the lottery or on Elvis's birthday?"

"No, we're not asking that."

"Well, what are you asking?"

"Just for *today*."

"What do you mean by that?"

"Could you stay clean and sober just for today?"

"Yes, of course."

"That's all we ask."

"What about tomorrow and the next day?"

"They aren't here yet. They don't exist. Do they? Or are we missing something?"

And so it began: a transformation. A journey of more than 30 wonderful years of having gone to clear, clean and sober living. A life transformed. Devoted. It was transformed within the warm confines of a single non-linear day. Today.

Chapter 75

A warrior overcoming grief

Has the time warrior used these principles to overcome grief… or at least to minimize it? Yes. Grief does not flow into a human heart directly from an event or a "loss," but rather from one's thoughts about that "loss." And so working with grief at the level of thought is very liberating.

If I "lose" someone I want to honor them rather than deepen the highly subjective sense of personal "loss." I want to respect them. I want to take the spotlight off of my own feelings and put it on the gift their life was to me. That practice truly honors the person who has passed, much more so than a prolonged emotional meltdown, which would be more about me-the-pitiable-griever than the person I am grieving. It would be more like a spoiled child's tantrum than an adult's love and respect for another person's life.

If I truly care about honoring the memory of my departed friend, I will not use their passing as a way to intensify the focus on myself and what I'm feeling.

Instead, I might consider being more creative than that.

Chapter 76

Why am I always choosing unavailable love partners?

Yes, why are you? I can't imagine a greater time waster! Not to mention passion-waster, love-waster and life-waster.

Our society and its various forms of entertainment—movies, novels, and so on—romanticize forbidden pleasures and illicit sexual affairs at the expense of true intimacy and faithful love.

We buy those exciting stories and start thinking that true romantic adventure can only be found down a dark, forbidden hallway. We say childish things like "The heart wants what it wants." Soon we are exciting ourselves over secret ecstasies and other self-defeating mind games. All made up to fill the void of an unfulfilling life.

Until, finally, as you can verify, it leads to way too much pain and sadness. Which it always does. But only every time, which is a bit of a sign from the universe that maybe we are on the wrong path.

Chapter 77

Fighting to remain focused

People tell me they are always "fighting to remain focused." They want to know how to hold that focus. How to win that stressful fight.

But it's the "fighting to remain focused" that is the problem.

Stop fighting.

Notice that when your eyes are looking at something far away the best way to bring the object into clear focus is to relax your eyes and let the object *come to you*. It's a gentle letting go of eye strain that brings an object into focus.

Focusing on a task is the same process: a relaxed experience in which you let yourself get drawn into the joy of the task and the energy that arises in the work. You let the task come to you and join with your energy and imagination.

And this merely takes practice.

It's not a character defect or personality problem we are dealing with here. Just as your inability to play a Chopin sonata on the piano is not a personality or character problem.

It's always and only a matter of practice.

Napoleon Hill had many brilliant insights about goal achievement and success. (He also left me cold with his opinions about women needing to be subservient to their men, and his weird "transmutation of sex drive." That's where his philosophies entered the Twilight Zone. Most philosophy is biography in disguise, and Hill proves that in both the good advice and the bad.) He wrote brilliantly about staying on the path and having your definite major purpose be what guides your day. His books opened my eyes to the power of sustained focus.

I now hold focusing on the task at hand to be a slow and sacred practice. When things like this are actually practiced (instead of fought off or forced in) they take on a gentle naturalness, a second nature, and after awhile this is not an issue for you at all, and you wonder where your head was at when you thought it was. Practice does that. It makes the unnatural natural.

Chapter 78

What's the point of labeling things as "impossible"?

I find it useful to do the impossible.

Because our minds—inappropriately—put way too many of our visions in that unreachable "impossible" category.

Soon everything exciting looks unreasonable, and the poor human is left with mediocrity and nothing more. He feels like he's playing it safe. But he's rather pathetic compared to the true magic inside him.

Therefore I will often have you stand up and describe your IMPOSSIBLE vision. Make sure it has previously existed in your mind as "impossible." I want to open that box in the brain where you put all the wonderful things you could be doing but won't, because you have given those things the demon brand: impossible.

Having you do the "impossible" tricks your mind into ignoring the label and taking action to actually DO the thing.

Once you've identified your impossible task, find someone to partner with. If you are going to take your life to the next quantum level, get a partner, coach or mentor to hold you accountable and support you in what you are up to. Don't make it be just about you. Have a higher purpose than that. Allow the two of you to focus on the *result* you want. And then enroll others. Expand, reach out, create and ask for what you want. Have fun doing the impossible.

Chapter 79

I'm worried about growing old

Not ever growing old would be one way to try to manage time.

But is it really a good thing to not grow old? Is it worthwhile to even think about these things when we could be living instead? Why contemplate approaching old age? Fear comes from contemplating the future.

Love, on the other hand, comes from present-moment active service. If you are swept up in pure, creative service you won't know what age you are. You won't care.

Practice everything you want to be good at no matter what age you think you are. Whether things go "according to plan" is far less important than *who you become* in the process. Practice taking on "problems" as intriguing and amusing challenges that fire you up.

Practice.

Have your life be your piano. Or your martial art lesson.

How do you get good at playing your life? Practice now. Not in the future. It's really the answer. It eliminates the whole growing old issue. You're too swept

up to worry about some number that our social
convention of "aging" tries to attach to your life.

Chapter 80

What if I don't have a life purpose?

Help some people! Get into action. Get involved. Your life's purpose can't always be "figured out" in advance. In fact, trying so hard to figure it out and figure out what purpose label fits you will often keep you from your life's purpose.

Purpose, in my experience, gets discovered in the heart while you're on the wing, when the heart is pumping and you are soaring. You don't see it ahead of time; you look back over your shoulder and there it is... trying to catch up with you! So fly.

And be flexible as you fly. Swing and expand. Limber up as you rise up. Dance through the clouds, sing and have some fun. Let success *find you* based on your incredible energy for serving. Don't chase *it*. It will always run from you. If you catch yourself chasing, turn around and fly in the other direction. Watch it try to catch *you*.

Chapter 81

What about boredom?

Nothing's ever boring if you are bold and adventurous enough to adopt the warrior's approach.

Things are only boring when you view them through the prism of worry and resentment.

A task is only boring when you secretly realize you are not really challenging yourself to the fullest. So practice becoming absolutely courageous in what you do. Scare yourself. Then take it up a notch tomorrow!

A friend sent me a great message he got from Robert Holden: LIVE NOW, PROCRASTINATE LATER.

To really live now there are two things I want to phase out of my life forever: (1) Resentments about the past and (2) Worries about the future.

These two activities, strengthened by repeated indulgence, are like hagfish. Hagfish? Many people don't know what hagfish are, but they are just like worries and resentments.

In the real, undersea world, hagfish are blind, slimy, deepwater eel-like creatures that dart into the orifices of their prey and devour them, alive, from the inside.

Kill the hagfish in your life. Then you can live now and maybe procrastinate later.

Chapter 82

Stay in the moment… Yes, this one

Every chance you get, become excited about the glorious present moment opportunity. Stay out of the past, unless you are dissolving past beliefs that drag you down.

And stay out of the future, unless you are LOVING drawing a map of it for yourself to follow. But even that's a present moment activity.

Love what you do now. Make today and only today your masterpiece.

Hire a moving van if you have to.

But bring everything home into today. Don't leave anything out there stranded in the future.

I experience a stressed-out feeling whenever I think about the deadline for a creative project. But my stress comes from having that project be in the future.

Non-linear time management doesn't allow that line that stretches into the future. Because the linear thought process always produces stress. Unreasonable stress.

Here's what always works for me. Creating my perfect *day*. Figuring out what I'd have to do in *one day* (today) to automatically meet the deadline.

So if my book is 220 pages, I know that if I write two pages a day I can finish it in less than five months (my deadline). So I have a new project. It isn't a book, it's two pages. Today. That's all I have to do, and it's all I ever have to worry about. Two pages. It's fun. It's exciting. And it's very satisfying.

Some days I get on a passionate roll and write ten pages! Nothing can stop me! So I'm way ahead of deadline. I can sometimes get ahead. I can never, ever—with this system—fall behind. It's a system called "today." I can never feel stress because I'm always working within my day. I don't stretch a linear line into the future.

Can you see it? Non-linear time management doesn't ever have a long timeline. It has two choices: now or not now.

Chapter 83

Sing for that good vibration

Playing piano is a way for me of getting unstuck. What it does is it breaks the barrier that comes between the conscious and the unconscious mind. The conscious mind wants to take over and refuses to let the unconscious mind work, the intuition. So if I can play the piano, that will break the block, and my intuition will be free to give things up to my mind, my intellect.

Madeleine L'Engle
(92 years old and author of over 60 books)

Ah, music. Doesn't it just get you there? I like to sing between coaching sessions or writing stints to harmonize myself with the vibratory nature of the universe and to return myself to joyful sanity. Laughing, Singing and Dancing are always three reliable paths home to our true nature. LSD for short.

You can read about spirit all you want, but music lets you experience it directly.

Singing one of my favorites, "Jailhouse Rock," I love the line, "If you can't find a partner use a wooden chair."

Reminds me of this observation by Michael Levin, who said, "From my experience with clients, I have found that wood is particularly good for absorbing fear and offering reassurance. Sitting on a wooden chair produces a subtly different effect than sitting on a metal chair. Stone is grounding, but unyielding earth has a hugely supportive effect. Walking barefoot strengthens everyone."

I like what he says. Except one thing. I don't like his assuming I will always have fear for my chair to absorb. Kind of like the book *Feel The Fear and Do It Anyway*— a book that assumes you'll always have a ton of fear— and which says you might as well **just feel it and override it** with a brave face. Or find a better chair.

What a struggle that is.

For most of my life I would have agreed with those assumptions of ever-present fear. But I now know from experience that the thoughts and beliefs that produce fear can be questioned and deleted and you can be in ever-increasing numbers of situations, fearless.

There's something about music that helps this process. When I'm inside the music, carried by the song, time is gone, and there is no fear of death. And, losing the fear of death, we experience the death of fear.

In the movie *First Knight,* Lancelot is approached by a man he has just defeated in a sword fight. The man asks Lancelot how to become a great warrior. Lancelot says, "You have to study your opponent, how he moves, so you know what he's going to do before he does it... You have to know *that one moment* in every fight, when you win or lose, and you have to know how to wait for it... **And you have to not care whether you live or die."**

Chapter 84

Don't my goals tie me to the future?

The more seriously you regard your deadlines and the more you keep your word on meeting your deadlines, the stronger you get internally. The higher your self-esteem becomes. The more you trust yourself.

If certain "goals" scare you (tie you to the future, same thing) don't use them. Keep re-writing them until they *excite* you. Goals are tools. They serve you. If they don't, use another tool. I wouldn't use a machine gun for pest control. I might try it once, but I'd probably choose something else after that.

An outcome goal is just a game you make up. You don't always win. That's actually what makes it fun. The possibility of losing. You can be very sincere about the game without being too serious.

Trust yourself. If an outcome goal doesn't serve you, drop it. But a commitment is different. A commitment is an internal promise you have made to yourself. I would not drop those. And I wouldn't make them casually.

Short-term doable process goals keep you focused. They insure action. That's why they are so effective at carrying you forward. Create a structure for yourself.

Then create a routine to follow. Develop a system that minimizes distraction.

Chapter 85

How do I deal with my ego?

If you have a healthy ego—designed by you for successful interaction with society and other egos—you can use it consciously to achieve goals and keep commitments. You can also preserve your spirit and soul in the process, being *in* this world but not *of* it.

Healthy egos are built with healthy self-esteem. To not keep a commitment to yourself lowers your self-esteem and self-trust. So practice keeping them. All it takes is practice.

People often struggle with their self-esteem. If you struggle, it is not useful to believe you lack some good quality. Like an inability to focus for a long time or an undisciplined personality.

It's not discipline that you struggle with because you have as much as any of us do. It's your story about yourself that has you struggle. I wrote *The Story of You* to share accounts of how people can see that it's the story—not reality—that's in your way.

People have a story that says they have very little influence over the results they get in life. Not a true story. Your life is created. It's not delivered to you.

You can *create* the future—through process-goal-setting and achievement—without *living* in the future. Just like studying a map before you go somewhere. Or looking at a menu before the meal. You don't walk on the map. You don't eat the menu. Once you've created your goal and project you set the future aside. You don't live there or even give it another thought. Just enjoy the present moment fully. That's a warrior's way with non-linear time.

If I want to play guitar like Clapton, I can start learning some chords today and realize that Clapton did this very thing, struggled to form these very first chords. So my vision of being Clapton is already happening *right now*.

Anything that has you stop or quit or get discouraged is always just a thought. Capture each negative thought or image on paper and work it. Challenge it. Go to war with it.

Challenging your own beliefs is very hard to do and takes more unflinching courage than anything I know of on this planet, but it also yields more immediate, amazing, beautiful-feeling rewards than anything I've experienced. The unexamined life is not worth living because our dreams are never realized in such a life.

My clients try to tell me (their story) that they are uniquely and personally not good at following through with things. I remind them that we are all imperfect at following through because we are human. No one is unique this way. So drop that story—it doesn't serve you—and look closely enough and you'll see a lot of examples in your life when it's not even true.

Process goals are impossible to fail at when executed and they require no follow-through. If one of your process goals is to walk two miles today, get out there and walk the miles. End of story. No more follow-through necessary.

Still have ego problems? Problems make you better, stronger, wiser and more creative. If we had a pill for that we'd all be addicted. Yet we demonize problems, run from them, and think they are awful and shouldn't be happening. We have a story of a future perfect world and it's a story that ruins the even better world right in front of us. It's the story that has you desiring something other than the opportunity in front of you. That desire is what keeps you from being a time warrior.

Don't use desire that way. Don't use it for longing and wishing. Use it for instant energy.

We don't always know how to desire effectively but we once did. Kids, especially the really young ones, really know how to desire. So it's in you. You were born with it. Then you added the negative stories. All those stories are untrue, but you believe they keep you safe.

They don't.

Here's how success happens: You create the project and you create the power. It's always down to you and back to you. And you can also choose *not* to create, and that's fine too if that's what you want. There will be no ego in any of that because pure action leaves the ego behind.

With no ego nagging you, you now get to make it all up. Now it's all made up, rather than being driven by your identity. There are no projects that are "right" for you until you say they are. And you can change your mind.

Now you're having fun creating new habits through practice. Playing the game differently. If your deadline is

Friday, you might play a game called "I'll do it by Thursday." It's all games anyway, so why not make up some that serve you instead of all the games you *imagine* are out there that scare you?

Chapter 86

How do I learn to trust that there will be abundance?

Why do you need to learn to trust? If you want to make scrambled eggs, do you need to first trust that the eggs will scramble?

You just make the eggs.

You don't walk around trying to trust the scrambling process first.

We add way too much to our minds. We burden ourselves in the mind.

While life waits.

You *could* just wake up and make the eggs. Very efficient. You can do the same with the economy. Just make money. Perform the service. Receive the money. And of course you can budget and save. That's a fun thing. They aren't mutually exclusive.

I wouldn't waste any further time trying to "trust the abundance of the universe." I would, instead, *test* it with action. Test whether it's abundant or not by serving people to such a degree that you finally know. (Spoiler alert: it is.)

Abundance! Everyone I know who really tests it, finds it. Much better than trying to believe in it.

Your mind and your intentions are there to serve you, not scare you. Learn to use your mind (more powerful than a thousand computers, plus it has imagination, insight and intuition) in a way that keeps you in action.

Chapter 87

Why do we hate rich people?

Once a friend told me she hated all rich people and found them to be "wasteful, arrogant and annoying."

I thought about what she said and then I told her I was hit upon the other day by a homeless guy who was wasteful, arrogant and annoying. Many poor people are. Many rich people are, too.

But what does that have to do with you? It is as relevant to your life as last year's lottery numbers.

All successful, productive people live in excess. Is that true? That's certainly not my experience. It's a story. Stories stop us from serving and living exciting lives.

Chapter 88

But how do I become creative?

All creativity emerges from inquiry. What would I like to create right now? What do I want to produce? What action can I take? Because inquiry always produces an Inquirer, your highest, most creative self. Without inquiry, you are in victim mode.

Once I choose what I'd like to create I am in action. Taking action is the little trick. It's far simpler than it looks. But we complicate it with stories and clinging like snails to negative beliefs about ourselves that we've built up over the years—none of which ever turns out to be really true.

All action has you leaving your comfort zone. That's what's fun about it when you do it—and scary when you think about it in advance.

Creativity is not about the mind, it's about the body, and the action that body takes. The mind just shows up later with a bundle of fresh new ideas. Ideas you'll enjoy acting on.

Chapter 89

How do I help my children with this?

Talk to your children about how the mind works. Ask them questions. Don't lecture.

But the key here is you, yourself.

Your children will learn more from *who you are being* than from what you are saying. Master life yourself. That's the greatest gift you can give your children.

Good luck having children that listen to your "advice." I've never known that to happen. Why would you want that anyway? Is that what *you* longed for as a child? Advice?

Your children will listen to who you *are*. So work on yourself. Drop the drama about your difficult past. Be proud of your time in hell.

Your problem is not your child—it's your expectation. What if he had his own life to live any way he wanted? What if he had freedom? (A life without psychic interference or negative thought-beams from you.) If I was your child that's what I would want. I would want you to love me, and be a good role model for me, even discipline me, but that would be all.

I would eventually want you to have a life of your own wherein you were emotionally independent and not mentally in my world all the time. That's what I would want.

Chapter 90

What if I want to get back at someone?

Ask yourself if what you are about to do is loving, creative and useful to your life.

If the answer is yes, move forward.

If the answer is no, change course.

If you are still looking to "get back at" someone, or if you are indulging some other infantile emotion, then take a deep breath and ask yourself better questions. Take a walk and try to wake up to the beauty of the universe instead of allowing yourself to stay trapped in obsessing about the behavior of others.

You can eliminate reacting and over-reacting entirely by shifting, always, to a true warrior's activities: creating and producing. Have your mind and body be energy fields that spend the day creating and producing. Phase out reacting-to-others completely.

Chapter 91

But what if life is still unfair?

I thought life was unfair for a long time. Full of boring work for me while others had fun.

Then I saw the real truth. Life was not unfair.

I was unfair.

I was unfair to myself for having it be okay with me to wallow passively in my victim mindset. I was cheating myself out of a beautiful, fulfilling life.

You can make *anything* sparkle with natural interest, because everything's inherently compelling in and of itself, until we inject it with negative thoughts and beliefs.

So *find* the fun and interest in the task! Or add it! Find it in yourself, and be both the director and the actor in your own play and direct yourself to do this task with great energy. You can do that.

Our problem is that we forget we can be the director and the actor. Instead, we pout like little children. We go on strike against life. Waiting for something entertaining to come and entertain us.

If we'd shift our thinking just a little we'd see what was really possible. We would attack life with humor and energy.

When you motivate others well it's because you have stepped outside yourself. The secret to self-motivation is that you can also step outside yourself and motivate yourself as a director motivates an actor. You can play both roles. Any time you want!

Chapter 92

But what about family distractions?

Many of the people I coach are frustrated by being pulled off-task by family members who demand their time.

They say they want to always be there for their family. They say, "Family comes first! Always!"

But then they don't accomplish what they're committed to accomplish and they become very discouraged.

If you do have something special to accomplish, *make time* for it, and be clever and compassionate about it, and your family will support and admire you for it. Or not. But that's their problem, not yours. You can love a family member dearly and not be at their beck and call every minute. Being "there for someone" all the time does not prove your love, it proves how little you respect their independence and your own priorities.

Make time for what *you* choose to do.

The best gift you can give others (even better than the highly overrated "empathy") is to have your own life work.

Chapter 93

How do I find my project?

People sometimes think "the knowing" of their next project descends upon them at some time. Or, that "the knowing" is in their DNA already. It is not.

The knowing is created. It's something you make up. You can make up what you want. You can invent a big purpose. It's all creation. (In fact, no one has ever had a definite major purpose that wasn't made up.)

Purpose is whatever you say it is when you wake up in the morning. And purpose doesn't carry over all by itself from day to day. You have to create it fresh when you wake up. And that's good news because it puts you in complete creative control.

If we all had a purpose that we "found" in a dream or in our hearts or under a mossy stone in the forest outside of Camelot, we wouldn't be creative. We wouldn't get to do the most fun thing in the whole world, and that is to create.

Chapter 94

Waking up feeling bad?

The only reason they come to see me
is that I know that life is great—
and they know I know it.

Clark Gable

A true time warrior takes up arms against depressed feelings and worrisome, fearful thoughts. She sees that they are never true anyway.

You do not need to wake up with a depressed or threatened feeling. That feeling, however vague, stark and lonely, can only be produced by something you are thinking and believing. It doesn't just arrive out of nowhere. Thought always comes before a feeling and *causes* the feeling.

So if I were waking up feeling anything other than happy and warlike, I would keep a pad of paper by the bed, and when I woke up I'd capture the thoughts that have me feeling down. I'd write them down. I'd work backwards if I had to; in other words, if I didn't "know" the thoughts, I'd put my feelings into words. I'd ask myself, "If my feelings could speak, what would they be saying?" Then I'd write that down.

Then I'd do Byron Katie's Work—her four questions and the turnarounds (www.thework.com)—on these thoughts every morning for two weeks running.

The only reason I'd do all this is because it works.
And all I'm doing with that work is creating a space in which life can become great again. That's life's true nature and I want to know it.

Give me space. Give me land (lots of land) under starry skies above. And I can whirl. Like the dervish poet Rumi. I can dance like Muhammad Ali. Float like a butterfly.

You need space for that. Stories bind you up and fence you in. Fears sweep in like the monkeys in *The Wizard of Oz*. Monkeys aren't supposed to fly, but the story-telling mind can make even little monkeys be evil fliers.

Stories! There's a story, for example, about what it means to be 66. In fact there are many stories to choose from about what it means to be 66. Some people say "60 is the new 40." Because people are living to be in their nineties now whereas they only used to live to be in their seventies. So 60 is the new 40! I'm only 46! Woo hoo!

But being 66 itself is just a story. Because truly my age is now! Am I alive now? Yes. (As I'm writing this I am. I may not be as you're reading this—and of course I'm referring to future generations who are reading this.)

Now or not now. Those are the two ages people have, really. I know people in their sixties who shuffle around like death warmed over and people in their nineties who wake up and run and dance and laugh and swim and sing and play. So it's really just now or not now.

Chapter 95

Stop all that thinking

Sometimes I take myself out of action so I can nurture and indulge some distended linear thinking about how weighed down I am by life's challenges (always in the future).

But then I visit my coach and he helps me see that on a very deep level it is impossible for me to be weighed down by life's challenges.

Unless I choose to think and believe I am weighed down. A kind of sick form of self-hypnosis.

In the end, it can only be my *thinking* that weighs me down. That's, in fact, the *only* thing that can *ever* weigh me down. My own thinking.

So for me to get back into the non-linear warrior zone I want to challenge and eliminate any thinking that is weighing me down.

So, now. What will lift me up? New thinking?

NO!

I need to stop all the thinking about thinking. Stop trying to replace negative thoughts with positive thoughts. All this thinking is overrated as a motivational force.

Doing, on the other hand, is underrated.
Doing is the most underrated thing there ever was.

Chapter 96

Earn first and spend later

When you spend first and earn later, which is one way to do it, you will never know how close to the financial line you are before you need to quit spending forever. (You're probably already there.)

We are a whole nation whose politicians sought reelection to their elite club by spending first and hoping you and I and our children and grandchildren would *earn later* to cover their vote-buying. (And to even call it "buying" is an undeserved compliment, because buying requires an exchange of value.)

Financial freedom comes from making tough-minded, courageous choices. It is not about going unconscious. The true economic optimist sees the possibilities and makes things happen *without* spending unearned money. That's the part financial optimism plays. It has you see options instead of obstacles.

Optimism is a tool for opening your thought and energy to new possibilities for action. It is not a result of outside circumstances.

Optimism is a tool for thinking that can be used any time. It is not a feeling. Most people think optimism is a feeling that comes and goes, and that's why they never know how to use it.

Optimism is an effective tool, like a shovel. Think how useful a shovel is if you are going to dig a hole in your yard. You never ask before you dig, "How do I get myself to feel like a person who uses a shovel?"

You use one or you don't.

Chapter 97

Use your fifteen minutes

Perseverance is not a long race;
it is many short races one after another.

Walter Elliott
The Spiritual Life

Andy Warhol's well-worn prediction was that in the future everyone would be famous for 15 minutes. Let's put some life into that and say that from now on you can be a successful person for 15 minutes... any and every 15-minute period you select!

Isaac Asimov was a bestselling science fiction writer of such classics as *I, Robot*, but he was even better known for how productive he was. He wrote over 500 books in many categories—mysteries, science, history, you name it—often writing 12 to 17 books in a single year.

No one has ever come close to his remarkable output of books. His key to success was his *readiness to write*. He never had to get ready to write. He never had to work on his motivation or procrastination. To a time warrior like Asimov, there were no such emotional luxuries as procrastination or lack of motivation.

He said, "It is important to be able to begin writing at any time. If there are 15 minutes in which I have nothing to do, that's enough to write a page or so."

Now let's go from 15 minutes to one minute. Spencer Johnson is the author of *The One Minute Sales Person.* "I have more fun," he said, "and enjoy more financial success, when I stop trying to get what I want and start helping other people get what they want." He can often do that in one minute!

He makes his book about a one-minute sales person because it only takes a minute to turn the whole focus around from me to you. I turn away from satisfying myself and turn toward making you happy. That's when sales happen.

That's when requests of any kind start to get answered in the positive. When my request honors your world—not mine. Focusing on my own "needs" will cause me to lose sales, lose friendships, lose business, lose happiness. Wanting something for myself is demeaning and always feels infantile at the level of soul. Wanting something for *you* is more fun than I ever dreamed it could be.

My success will come once I'm ready—truly, always ready—to use any 15 minutes that shows up to *serve somebody* with.

Chapter 98

What, exactly, do I want to do?

I've got more energy now than when I was younger
because I know exactly what I want to do.

George Balanchine
Ballet master

Push my head under the water and I experience an increase in energy because I am immediately focused on what I want to do. I want to get out of the water. So I know *exactly* what I want to do.

And any time I know exactly what I want to do my energy increases.

My energy increases the same way the sun's power increases when I take the diffuse rays and harness them and focus them through a simple magnifying glass and let the focused ray of sun burn an old dead leaf like a science fiction laser.

When we *focus* we are joining the energy that created the world. We forget that we can always do that. We forget, and then we cling to worries and fears and all the mindstuff that keeps us passive. Soon anger emerges. A vicious circle.

But the minute someone calls us out back to play volleyball or take a swim or climb a mountain or ride a bike, something happens. We are breathing deeply once again! We are joining the energy that created the world. Breathe first, then let the mind expand. Don't wait for it to happen the other way around.

Chapter 99

Stop lying to yourself

People want their lives to be different. People want success instead of failure. But then people begin sentences with "I don't know how to..." and right then they are down the rabbit hole. They have become victims. The primary thought of a victim is "I don't know how to." And it's always a lie.

People tell me, "I want to be a coach, but I don't know how to..." Whatever. And why would I want to help a liar like that? My book about the 17 lies was about that whole false approach to life. A toxic mind swamp of self-deceiving. (I only know it because I did it myself... but only for 40 years.)

If you want to be a coach, coach. If you want to be a singer, sing. If you want to be a writer, write. If you want some money, go ASK for it and serve someone. Notice the common thread here. And I repeat this quote again by Aristotle: "Whatever we learn to do, we learn by actually doing it. People come to be builders, for instance, by building, and harp players by playing the harp. In the same way, by doing just acts we come to be just. By doing self-controlled acts, we come to be self-controlled, and by doing brave acts we become brave."

A warrior doesn't have to "know" what to do. A warrior doesn't have to "know how to" do something. A warrior simply *chooses* to do it.

Chapter 100

How do you make life meaningful?

That's a question I was asked by a wonderful woman named Sophie Chiche, who was editing a book on the meaning of life. She already had submissions from Nelson Mandela, Deepak Chopra, Wayne Dyer and many other famous people and wanted me to write a page myself. Was she sure about that?

How do I keep my life meaningful? And what method or system do I use to *stay engaged* in the meaningful aspects of life?

I wrote to her that "meaning" is what my mind plays with when my body has nothing to do.

I find I can add meaning and significance to *anything* and then just as quickly subtract it! So what's the actual point?

Each time it's just a naming game in my mind. And in no case is any "true" meaning established for me beyond the naming game. Why have this outer thing called "life" that I'm trying to "stay engaged with" by adding meaning to it?

Looking anxiously outside like that is a waste of time. The warrior looks within.

Jesus said the kingdom of heaven is *within*. Marcus Aurelius said, "Dig within. Within is the wellspring of good; and it is always ready to bubble up, if you just dig."

So, how to stay engaged?

Friedrich Nietzsche once observed that "Man is the only animal who has to be encouraged to live." I've needed that encouragement myself in past days and suicidal nights gone by.

And one day I no longer needed it. One day I discovered that my encouragement was found by digging within! Those dark days and nights were gone for good and the blue was back in the sky. The long, dreary linear life was over and I saw how short this vertical uprising called living could be! I mean it was already over! Who needs to be encouraged to maintain something that's already over?

And in that same spirit, were I to find myself needing "help to stay engaged" in this life I would know it's time to call the hotline once again.

It's only when my mind is contaminated with fearful beliefs that I try to add meaning to things. But that activity is always (as the Zen masters say) like adding legs to a snake. Like painting a rose with red paint.

The great mythologist Joseph Campbell was once asked by an up and coming writer what Campbell would recommend as a cure for writer's block. "Cut off your head," said Campbell.

In other words, write from the heart, live from the heart. We are always and already totally engaged. We breathe in from life and breathe out to life and this mutual giving keeps us engaged. It is the very definition of engagement.

Charlie Manson thought there was *secret meaning* in the Beatles' *White Album*, especially in the song "Helter Skelter." People have insisted to me that when Jesus says, in the Bible, that some men, if they behave certain ways, are better off at the bottom of the ocean with a millstone around their necks, there is a subtle symbolic "meaning" there that I might be missing. Something more spiritually elegant than "I'd like to drown them."

Only the mind that believes the darkest of superstitions can talk the body into feeling disengaged from this whirling life. So if I believe I need a *method* that helps me to stay engaged, I am like Nietzsche's man who needs to be encouraged to stay alive.

That's not for me anymore.

I like staying alive in exactly the same way the Bee Gees like stayin' alive.

Chapter 101

What will set me free?

Van Gogh said, "If you hear a voice within you saying 'I am not a painter,' then, by all means, paint... and that voice will be silenced."

If you hear a voice saying, "I'm not very organized," then organize your desk, and that voice will also be silenced.

People who think they are "not very organized" don't have to re-experience childhood with better parents, find better medications, or take some long time-management course. What they need to do is organize.

That's the non-linear approach. Just organize. The linear approach is to string the problem out over time. To put yourself though lots of linear paces as you struggle to finally "know how to" organize your desk.

The more successful you are the more joyously complicated your external life can get. (More people want your time. Don't forget: it's something you used to pray for!) The organizing system that worked for you last year will not work now because more people are clamoring for you. You become more valuable to them the better you get at what you do. But your life can get more complicated in the process.

Unless you are a warrior and see it coming.

If my professional life is to be simple, I must simplify it myself each day, each week. I must simplify it by organizing it. Putting things in compartments so they don't haunt me like ghosts.

The greatest drain on my energy is an unfinished task. The way to restore my energy is to DO that task or SEAL IT OFF inside a compartment of time on my calendar so my mind can be free of it. A free mind succeeds faster.

I recently enjoyed a very powerful article in *Sports Illustrated* about college football's Owen Marecic of Stanford who plays both ways, fullback and linebacker. He is an extraordinary player who operates from an unmovable commitment to being a warrior with his time. He organizes his time and energy better than other players do.

Marecic's coach, Jim Harbaugh, keeps on his office desk one of the several helmets Marecic has cracked while at Stanford. (Extreme focus.) At Harbaugh's request, Marecic signed the helmet, along with the words he lives by:

TODAY
GIVE
ALL
THAT
YOU
HAVE,
FOR
WHAT
YOU
KEEP
INSIDE
YOU LOSE FOREVER

There is something better than heaven, and it is not hell. It is the eternal, meaningless, creative mind. It cannot stop for time or space or even joy. It is so brilliant it will shake what's left of you into the depths of all-consuming ecstasy.

Byron Katie

About the Author

Steve Chandler is a world-famous personal success coach to people from all walks of life, including bestselling authors, public speakers, CEOs and media personalities, small business owners, university faculty and leaders, major account salespeople and the world's top business and life coaches.

As a corporate trainer he has worked with over thirty Fortune 500 companies and more than 600 other organizations in the areas of goal achievement, ownership culture, and sales and leadership. He has also served as a fundraising consultant and trainer to non-profits and is the co-author of the bestselling *Relationshift: Revolutionary Fundraising.*

Chandler is also a nationally recognized keynote speaker with over 1,000 speeches given throughout the U.S. and Canada. He is the creator and leader of two year-long Steve Chandler Mastermind groups and five Steve Chandler Coaching Schools for top-level business coaches, marketing consultants and life coaches. He has also served as a visiting teacher and lecturer at the University of Santa Monica graduate program in Soul-Centered Leadership and as a special guest coach on the award-winning TV reality program *Starting Over*.

Chandler is the author and co-author of dozens of books, including the bestsellers, *100 Ways to Motivate Yourself, Reinventing Yourself, 100 Ways to Motivate*

Others, *17 Lies That Are Holding You Back* and *Fearless*. His books have been translated into more than 40 foreign-language editions. He is the creator and writer of the popular blog iMindshift.com.

Chandler is a graduate of both the University of Arizona (Creative Writing and Political Science) and the elite Defense Language Institute, Presidio of Monterey, California (Russian language). He is a Cold War veteran, with four years of military service at the U.S. Army Security Agency in Berlin, Germany, and Psychological Warfare at Fort Bragg, North Carolina.

Chandler lives outside of Phoenix, Arizona, and can be reached at www.stevechandler.com.

Recommended Websites

Steve Chandler: www.stevechandler.com

Club Fearless: www.clubfearless.net

Steve Hardison: www.theultimatecoach.net

Deuce Lutui: www.tbolitnfl.com

I Mind Shift (The Chandler Blog): www.imindshift.com

Byron Katie: www.thework.com

Also by Steve Chandler

RelationShift: Revolutionary Fundraising
(with Michael Bassoff)
100 Ways to Motivate Yourself
Reinventing Yourself
17 Lies That Are Holding You Back
50 Ways to Create Great Relationships
100 Ways to Create Wealth (with Sam Beckford)
The Small Business Millionaire (with Sam Beckford)
9 Lies That Are Holding Your Business Back
(with Sam Beckford)
Business Coaching (with Sam Beckford)
Two Guys Read Moby Dick (with Terrence N. Hill)
Two Guys Read the Obituaries (with Terrence N. Hill)
Two Guys Read Jane Austen (with Terrence N. Hill)
Two Guys Read the Box Scores (with Terrence N. Hill)
The Hands Off Manager (with Duane Black)
The Story of You
100 Ways to Motivate Others (with Scott Richardson)
10 Commitments to Your Success
The Joy of Selling
Fearless
The Woman Who Attracted Money
Shift Your Mind: Shift the World

Audio Programs by Steve Chandler

The following audio programs are available from
www.SteveChandler.com in downloadable mp3 format:

9 Lies Audio Companion
10 Habits of Successful Salespeople
17 Sales Lies
Are You a DOER or a FEELER?
Challenges
Choosing
Client Acquisition Part One: Referrals
Creative Relationships
Expectation vs. Agreement
Financially Fearless
How to Help a Pessimist
How to Solve Problems
Is It a Dream or a Project?
Making a Difference
Ownership and Leadership
People People
Purpose vs. Personality
SERVING vs. PLEASING People
The Focused Leader
The Function of Optimism
The Joy of Succeeding: Steve Chandler LIVE in LA
The Owner / Victim Choice
The Ultimate Time Management System

The Fearless Mindset
The How To vs. The Want To
Welcoming Every Circumstance
Who You Know vs. What You Do
You'll Get What You Want By Asking for It

MindShift: The Steve Chandler Success Course
Read by Steve Chandler
(total playing time: 9 hours, 25 minutes)

Shifting to a higher level of success takes much more than "information." It requires a leap in understanding that changes how you view the world... a *MindShift*.

MindShift, Part One. (62 minutes) 1. Open Mind
2. The Ladder to Spirit 3. From Reaction to Creation
4. Exiting the Comfort Zone 5. Dissolving Expectation

MindShift, Part Two. (62 minutes) 1. Commitment
2. RelationSHIFT 3. Create Your Own Space

MindShift, Part Three. (50 minutes) 1. Precise vs.
Vague 2. Logic Power 3. Creating Unfair Advantages

MindShift, Part Four. (53 minutes) 1. Create a Physical
Equivalent 2. Replacing Old Habits with New 3. The
Magic of the End User 4. Getting OUT of the Future
5. The Terminator 6. Weakness into Strength

MindShift, Part Five. (45 minutes) 1. Secret Power of
Practice 2. Fearlessness 3. Personality Prison

MindShift, Part Six. (40 minutes) 1. Introducing Spirit 2. Commitment and Spirit 3. Spiritual Muscle 4. Doing Things Religiously

MindShift, Part Seven. (44 minutes) 1. Money Fear 2. My Calling 3. Using the 80/20 Formula

MindShift, Part Eight. (47 minutes) 1. Busy-ness is Laziness 2. Laziness is Cowardice 3. Self-concept is Destiny 4. Re-design Your Self-esteem

MindShift, Part Nine. (52 minutes) 1. Creating Agreements 2. Language of Success 3. The Owner-Victim Distinction 4. Owner Words vs. Victim Words

MindShift, Part Ten. (46 minutes) 1. Proper Use of Heroes 2. The "How To" vs. the "Want To" 3. Creating Your Success as A Creator

MindShift bonus audio: The Back Story: My Life Was A Disaster - Steve Chandler in conversation with Julie Blake. (64 minutes)
Steve reveals to interviewer Julie Blake the details of his personal journey from bankruptcy, divorce and addiction to a joyful, creative and prosperous life. This bonus audio is only available with the purchase of MindShift.

73⊃   254
2825   8457

CPSIA information can be obtained at www.ICGtesting.com
Printed in the USA
LVOW07s1140130915

453974LV00003B/505/P

9 781600 250378